STILL SHINING!

Discovering Lost Treasures from the 1904 St. Louis World's Fair

by DIANE RADEMACHER

For Jane,
Enjoy the fair that was –
and is "still shining."
Best Wishes,
Diane Stademacher

March 2, 2006

Still Shining! Discovering Lost Treasures from the 1904 St. Louis World's Fair

ISBN: 1-891442-20-1
Library of Congress Control Number: Pending
Published by
Virginia Publishing Co.
P.O. Box 4538
St. Louis, MO 63108
(314) 367-6612   www.stl-books.com

VIRGINIA PUBLISHING CO.

Still Shining

Dedication

To Dad — Who saw the fair through the eyes of a baby

To Mom — Who loved Dad and kept the fair memory alive

To Charleen — For your inspiration, encouragement and assistance

To Ralph — For discovering the fair treasure that sparked the idea

To Ron — Who loved to share the shining memories of the fair

And Thank You, Lord.

Author's Note and Acknowledgments

Still Shining! originated to answer a twofold question continually asked about the 1904 St. Louis World's Fair: Why was it torn down and is anything left? Herein lies part of the answer. The pages that follow rediscover some of the splendid treasures of the fair and where they are located today. To qualify for inclusion in the book, the building or exhibit item needed to be located in a place generally accessible to the public, or viewable from the street or at a distance (in the case of fair buildings converted to private residences). Exploring these treasures today generates a momentary "I was there" experience for a reconnection to that fabulous fair.

It is my hope that my family and friends who helped make this book possible see their ideas and contributions reflected in its pages and share in its accomplishment.

Heartfelt thanks to my wonderful family:

Charleen and Ralph Sartori, for your love, inspiration, support — and for uncovering the first unique fair treasure.

Richard, Kathy, Abby and Mary Kate Sartori; Joe, Debra, Danielle and Joshua Sartori; Sherri, Rob, Jacob and Andy Mitchell; and Julie, Bob, Sophie and Fiona Curran — for your love and encouragement. Special kudos to Joe Sartori for early editing and great ideas.

Many thanks to my friends and members of the 1904 World's Fair Society for their kindness and assistance during this long-term effort:

Max and Shara Storm, for sharing a wonderful collection of memorabilia and an incredible source of fair information; Yvonne Suess, for treasure hunting, stereoviews, and photography; Nancy Schuster, for last-minute photography and editing; Barbara Uhl, for photography and preparing the index; Mike Truax and William Seibert, for technical proofreading; Barbara Schira, Steve and Lauren Schira, and Karen and Mike Harper, for the long-term loan of my dear friend Ron Schira's extensive fair library.

Marcia Haley (my ever-patient and witty traveling buddy), Mary Ann Dill, Louise Drescher, Msgr. Edward Eichor, Phyllis Kent, Jo Ann Sander, and Pat Villmer, for participating in unique trips to seek out fair treasures in St. Louis and across the country.

Mary Jane Belanger, Hugh and Ann Bergman, Terry and John Blaskiewicz, Margaret "Cookie" Browning, Bob and Sally Bryant, John and Carol Bush, Carol Diaz-Granados, Mark Eisenberg, Ron Garland, Philip Geerling, Jack Greaney, Jim Greensfelder, Ed Gurney, Fran Hamilton, Bobbie and Bob Herman, Mark Leahy, Reneé Murphy, Pat and Craig Osterberg, Bill and Jane Pieber, Mary Parker-Biby, Melanie Raffel, Glenn and Rosanne Sartori, Kelly Smith, Carl and Myrtle Speiser, and Ray and Sue Steinnerd for discovering fair treasures, sharing related information, and providing photographs.

Thanks also to the following information sources for invaluable help in researching the treasures from the fair: 1904 World's Fair Society (St. Louis, Missouri), Missouri Historical Society, St. Louis City Public Library, Missouri Botanical Garden, University City Public Library (Sue Rehkopf, Historical Society of University City), Washington University Library and Archives, St. Louis Art Museum (Norma Sindelar, archivist), St. Louis County Parks (Esley Hamilton, historic preservationist), St. Louis Zoo, Smithsonian Institution, Metropolitan Museum of Art (New York), Yale University, McPherson County Old Mill Museum (Lindsborg, Kansas; Lenora Lynam, archivist), Anheuser-Busch Archives, Cahokia Courthouse State Historic Site, El Reno Carnegie Library (El Reno, Oklahoma), University of Missouri–Columbia Archives, University of Louisville Archives, The Walters Art Museum (Baltimore, Maryland), Musée Rodin (Paris), Birmingham Historical Society, Southeast Missouri State University Museum and Archives, Elisabet Ney Museum (Austin, Texas), Clay County Missouri Historical Society, Cole County Missouri Historical Society, Cairo Illinois Public Library, Kansas City Missouri Parks and Recreation Department, The Corning Museum of Glass (Corning, New York), The Field Museum (Chicago, Illinois), Marjorie McNeely Conservatory at Como Park (St. Paul, Minnesota; Roberta Sladky, curator), Milwaukee Public Museum, Mercantile Library (St. Louis, Missouri), Missouri Mansion Preservation, Inc., National Mississippi River Museum and Aquarium (Dubuque, Iowa), Rock Island Arsenal Museum (Rock Island, Illinois), Sitka National Historic Park (Sitka, Alaska), Toledo Museum of Art, Independence National Park (Philadelphia, Pennsylvania), St. Louis Rowing Club (Karl J. Heilman, President, St. Louis Rowing Foundation), Atascadero Parks and Recreation Commission (Atascadero, California; Susan Beatie, public art advocate), and the Madison County Historical Society (IL), Inc.

Special thanks to Jeff Fister and the talented and creative Virginia Publishing staff who produced this book. Jeff's initial interest in the topic was a motivating force and his great ideas never ceased. I'm grateful to him for the opportunity to give readers a chance to reconnect to those shining days of the 1904 World's Fair through the tangible links presented in this book.

Foreword

In the opening decade of the twentieth century, the world turned its attention toward St. Louis, site of the largest world's fair in history, known as the Universal Exposition of 1904. The fair's purpose was to celebrate the centennial of the purchase of the Louisiana Territory by the United States from France. With the world poised on the brink of the age of electricity, people from all corners of the globe converged to share their cultures. Many of them experienced things they had never even dreamed of: entire buildings illuminated by electric lights, automobiles, moving pictures, baby incubators, elephants, flush toilets, ice cream cones. Fair President David R. Francis conveyed the scope of the fair by writing, "So thoroughly did it [the fair] represent the world's civilizations, that if all man's other works were by some unspeakable catastrophe blotted out, the records established at this Exposition by the assembled nations would afford the necessary standards for the rebuilding of our entire civilization."

And then it was over. The spectacular fair that had run from April 30 to December 1 was no more.

When the lights went out for the last time, emotions ran high. Twenty thousand people who had lived and worked on the grounds of the fair knew that they would need to find new living quarters as well as new jobs. Performers knew that they would lose their audiences. Owners of hotels and rooming houses knew that they would lose their clientele. Workers from foreign lands thought of returning to their respective countries and reuniting with family and friends.

Despite the changes that were about to occur in their lives, all of these people — and the nearly twenty million visitors to St. Louis and the Louisiana Purchase Exposition — would forever remember their days at the fair.

Today, one hundred years later, we still find ourselves singing "Meet Me in St. Louis" and replaying the popular movie of the same name. It is part of our culture, and for us St. Louisans it is part of us. When we walk in Forest Park, where the great fair stood, we can observe the few remaining structures and try to imagine the splendor that once was there. But we want more.

Thomas Jefferson, who authorized the Louisiana Purchase in 1803, wrote in a letter to his friend John Adams in 1817, "A morsel of genuine history is a thing so rare as to be valuable."

In *Still Shining!*, Diane Rademacher provides us with a rare morsel of history indeed. She spent more than two decades tracking down remnants from the fair — buildings, statues, exhibits. She traveled thousands of miles and interviewed scores of people. Her work provides us with specific information about vestiges of the greatest exposition the world has ever known.

During this centennial year, interest in this monumental event, which many people believe to be the pinnacle of St. Louis history, is at an all-time high. Is it any wonder that we are interested in learning about original items from the fair? They provide a tangible connection to the fair that we hold so dear.

Through this book you can share the excitement that Diane felt as she located these relics from the 1904 World's Fair. As you experience her passion for the fair, you'll know that the fair's legacy is still shining.

Max Storm

Founder, 1904 World's Fair Society
Co-Author, *1904 Olympic Games, Official Medals and Badges*

Table of Contents

Dedication 3
Author's Note and Acknowledgments 4
Foreword by Max Storm, Founder of the 1904 World's Fair
	Society 6
Photo Credits..9

Introduction
When the Lights Went Out 11
So Much to See – Maps of the Fairgrounds 14
The Fabulous Fair 16

Chapter One: Buildings and Structures
White Hall – Connecticut State Pavilion 30
Warm and Wonderful – The American Radiator Building 32
Permanent – The Palace of Art 34
Wee Bungalow – Nevada State Pavilion 37
Frontier Justice – Cahokia Courthouse 38
Under the Domes – West Virginia State Pavilion 40
Spreading the Word – The Press Building 42
Older Than Oklahoma – Oklahoma Territory Pavilion 44
Hardscrabble – General Grant's Cabin 46
For the Birds – 1904 Flight Cage 48
Foursquare – Utah State Pavilion 50
English Domestic Style – Wisconsin State Pavilion 51
Palace of Pines and Maples – Buildings of the Japanese
	Imperial Garden 52
The Secret Garden – Rhode Island State Pavilion 54
Homestead on the Range – The Swedish Pavilion..............56
Buildings on the Quadrangle and Beyond – Washington
	University 58

Chapter Two: Sculpture and Statuary
The Stroke of the Pen – *Signing of the Treaty* 68
Just to Think – Rodin's *The Thinker* 70
Revolutionary Disciplinarian – *Baron Friedrich Wilhelm von
	Steuben* 72
At the Gates – *Fountain Angel* 73
Birmingham's Giant on the Hill – *Vulcan* 74
Copies of the Classics – Gerber-Houck Statuary Collection ...76
Looking Homeward – *Forest Devotion* 78
Center Court – Meet Me at *The Eagle* 79
Southern Honors – *General Albert Sidney Johnston Memorial* 80
Water Nymphs – *The Wrestling Bacchantes* 82
Healing Waters – *Apollo* 84
Holding Back the Waters – *The Hewer* 85
Galloping for Gold – *The Mares of Diomedes* 86
Silent Music – *The Florentine Singer* 87
Treasures from the Orient – Japanese Eagle and Vase 88

Chapter Three: Exhibit Items ... and More
Expansion and Education – Thomas Jefferson's Headstone ...92
From Palace to Pub – Chandeliers at O'Connell's 95
Lighting the Way – Snow-viewing Lanterns from the
	Japanese Imperial Garden 96
The One and – "Owney" 98
Clear the Way – Snagboat Horatio G. Wright 100
Fit for Royalty – Prince Pu Lun Coach 101
Foreign Lights – French and Belgian Chandeliers 102
Top of the Line – Gorham Martelé Silver 104
Golden Fossil of the Fair – Gingko Tree 105

Big Time – The Floral Clock 106

Still the Grandest – World's Largest Pipe Organ 108

A Life for Others – St. Elizabeth Mosaics 110

The Solitary Column – Minnesota Shaft 111

Ring Out Freedom – The Liberty Bell 112

All that Sparkles – Libbey Cut Glass 114

Native North Americans – Vancouver Island Community ...115

Highlighting the Past – Japanese Garden Lanterns at Como
        Park 116

Carved Chronicles – Alaska's Totem Poles 118

Write Here – Presidential Desk 120

Rescued – Missouri Suite of Furniture 121

Monument to a Mayor – Obelisk from the Fair 122

To Defend – Department of War Display 123

A Visitor from the Jurassic Age – A Dinosaur at the Fair 124

1904 Olympian Games – Olympic Venues 125

In Conclusion 129

Legacies 130
Treasures by State 132
About the Author..133
Bibliography / Credits 134
Index 140
Contacts 143

Photo Credit Sources

The source of each photograph is identified by collection, book or photographer, except for the following books that are cited by author or publisher:

(Bayne) James Bayne Company, *Memories of the Louisiana Purchase Exposition*, 1904.

(Bennitt) Mark Bennitt (ed.), *History of the Louisiana Purchase Exposition*, 1905.

(Bennitt/1904 LPE CD), Mark Bennitt (ed.), *History of the Louisiana Purchase Exposition*, 1905 on CD-ROM. Adapted to digital media by Philip Geerling, Dynamic Solutions, St. Charles, MO, 2000 (1904 Louisiana Purchase Exposition CD).

(Buel) J.W. Buel (ed.), *Louisiana and the Fair*, 1904 - 1905.

(Francis) David R. Francis, *The Universal Exposition of 1904*, 1913.

(Official Photographic Co.) *Official Louisiana Purchase Exposition* (photo book), The Official Photographic Co., 1904.

(Rau) William H. Rau (Managing Director), *The World's Fair Comprising the Official Photographic Views of the Universal Exposition Held in St. Louis in 1904*, 1904.

When the Lights Went Out

*"No," Tootie said. "They will never
tear it down. It will be like this forever."*
Meet Me in St. Louis

(Official Photographic Company) Ronald E. Schira Collection

Festival Hall and the Cascades illuminated

A s midnight struck on December 1, 1904, Louisiana Purchase Exposition President David R. Francis cast the St. Louis World's Fair into fond memory as he performed the heart-rending task of closing that fabulous celebration. When he raised his hands in one last tribute to the brilliant spectacle before him, he fondly bid, "Farewell, a long farewell to all thy splendor." He threw the switch that extinguished thousands of lights as the band played "Auld Lang Syne" to the hushed crowd of one hundred thousand. A barrage of fireworks lit the panorama for the final encore before the radiant fairgrounds faded forever into the darkness. The fair that had transformed Forest Park into a magical kingdom for seven months was over, but the fair that transformed St. Louis continues to live in the legacies and memories wrought by that remarkable event, and in the splendid treasures that remain.

The city ordinance that granted the use of Forest Park for the Louisiana Purchase Exposition specified that the Exposition Company must clear the land and restore it to park use within one year of the closing date. Demolition of the fair, the largest ever held, was a monumental task. Bids were requested and the contract was awarded to the Chicago House Wrecking Company. For $450,000, the Exposition Company sold all of the mammoth exhibit palaces and buildings with their fixtures (except for the Art Palace, state and foreign government buildings, the fairgrounds railway system, selected statuary, midway attractions, and concession stands). Considering that fair construction costs approached $50 million, the salvage bid seemed a paltry sum. Nevertheless, the Exposition Company accepted the contract considering the labor costs involved to remove the huge palaces and buildings, and to recycle the materials.

Dismantling commenced immediately to meet the March 1905 deadline for the removal of displays. Most exhibits were packed away by January 31, 1905. The Chicago House Wrecking Company began its work to demolish and to remove eleven large exhibit palaces within six months. Enormous quantities of salvageable materials in excellent condition were made available for purchase and reuse. The wrecking company printed a catalogue advertising the reclaimed materials for sale. It listed one hundred million linear feet of lumber, "enough to build outright over ten (10) cities with a population each of 5,000 inhabitants," new steel roofing, doors, windows, sills, pipe with fittings, stoves, office equipment, and construction materials of all types. Many homes in Missouri and Arkansas were framed and finished using fair salvage. Three hundred and fifty thousand incandescent lamps were offered at 16 cents if new and 6 cents if used. Staff, the composition of plaster and hemp that was molded into the fanciful designs of the exhibit palaces, was practically valueless. Mountains of it were available for reprocessing or were disposed of in the park and at dump sites in the St. Louis area. Some materials were offered free if hauled away. Local citizens scavenged materials or just came to watch the demolition for one last peek at the vanishing fair.

**Chicago House Wrecking Catalogue
1904 World's Fair salvage**

Relocation rather than destruction was the happy fate of several of the smaller state and foreign buildings. Capable of being dismantled into sections, they were transported by rail and reconstructed all or in part as homes, or for educational and community purposes. Some exhibits, or parts thereof, were donated to the city or sold to local and national buyers. China gave its entire $135,000 pavilion to David R. Francis. Several notable artifacts in the collections of St. Louis' cultural institutions and businesses find their historic roots at the 1904 World's Fair. Many other treasures that were loaned for use at the fair were returned for display at sites throughout the country and overseas.

Concessions on the Pike, the midway and entertainment district at the fair, were costly to dispose of, impossible to sell, and even difficult to give away. At one point there was a short-lived proposal to retain the Pike as an amusement area. It was to be enhanced with a beach, illuminated tower, sports stadium, and playground, all within the shadow of the fair's simulated mountain range, the Tyrolean Alps. The plan was abandoned after nearby Washington University opposed it as an unwanted distraction for students and staff.

A new St. Louis tradition begins in the aftermath of the fair … sledding on Art Hill.

The Great Observation Wheel met its final fate at the end of the fair, but its demise gave rise to an urban legend that has bewildered St. Louisans for years. Originally slated for relocation to Coney Island in New York, plans fell through and the wheel was scheduled for destruction. Using dynamite, the demolition contractor reduced the once-great ride to a pile of twisted steel. While the tangled debris was removed in advance of park restoration, carting away the massive seventy-ton axle was a different story. The ensuing legend surrounding the whereabouts of the axle has become an unsolved mystery, generating scientific search efforts as well as speculation on the location of the massive axis around which thrills and memories once revolved.

On October 11, 1904, a committee was formed to oversee the restoration of Forest Park. George Kessler was appointed the Director of Restoration. He envisioned the redesign of the parklands to "hint frequently of the past grandeur of the exposition, but at the same time to conceal all evidence of man in the making of the pictures." The timeframe for restoration was extended and completed by 1908. Kessler's vision endured as vestiges of the fair remained apparent on the park's landscape for years. His perspective is still honored today as welcome renovations to the park's Grand Basin, a century after the fair, recall the design and splendor during the fabulous celebration.

There are numerous treasures and remnants, survivors of the fair, that hearken back to its glory days. They are scattered near and far and the following pages give a glimpse of the grandeur that was the 1904 St. Louis World's Fair.

So Much to See — Maps of the Fair

BIRD'S-EYE VIEW OF THE FAIR—The wonderful Cascades, with Festival Hall and the picturesque Gardens—the Palaces of Art, Education, Electricity, Agriculture, Machinery, Transportation, and Varied Industries, the Administration, Government and State edifices, arise as distant dreams of beauty and power. A mantle of silence is thrown over the merry din of the cosmopolitan Pike, and its weird spectaculars are hidden from view.

The Bird's-Eye View is only the skeleton of the vast creation of man which commemorates the transfer of a great territory only a century ago.

Bird's Eye View

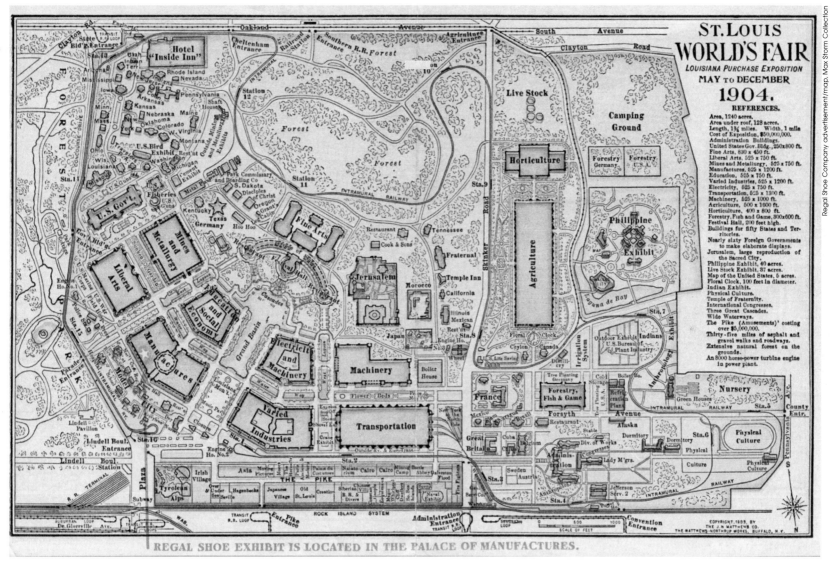

REGAL SHOE EXHIBIT IS LOCATED IN THE PALACE OF MANUFACTURES.

Fair "Floor Plan"

The Fabulous Fair

It was successful beyond expectations, it was a fabulous celebration, and its legacy is etched in the collective memory of the host city — St. Louis' 1904 World's Fair. St. Louis showcased itself and the products and progress of the world when in 1904, it held the largest fair ever, known officially as the Louisiana Purchase Exposition. For seven magical months, the world came to St. Louis to exhibit in and to marvel at the virtual kingdom created on the fairgrounds in the city's Forest Park. Expansive boulevards and scenic waterways connected ornate palaces and hundreds of unique buildings that displayed the achievements of mankind at the beginning of the twentieth century. Fairgoers came to see, to learn, and to just have fun — and took away the memories of a lifetime.

Missouri Historical Society

1904 World's Fair billboard

During the last part of the nineteenth century, international fairs gained popularity as major cities used them to demonstrate technological progress, to advertise products, and to promote commerce as the result of the Industrial Revolution. Fairs in the United States, most notably the Centennial Exposition of 1876 in Philadelphia and the Columbian Exposition in 1893 in Chicago, were also held to celebrate, in part, significant historical events. St. Louis followed that tradition. After losing out to Chicago for the Columbian Exposition, the city looked to host a fair in 1903 to commemorate the centennial of the Louisiana Purchase, Jefferson's acquisition of the huge tract of land west of the Mississippi from France that doubled the size of the young nation. For the bargain price of $15 million, thirteen states were subsequently carved out of that expanse with St. Louis strategically perched on the eastern border, just south of the confluence of the mighty Missouri and Mississippi rivers. The Louisiana Purchase is considered a significant milestone in the growth of the country, second only to the American Revolution, and St. Louis chose to commemorate it.

(Buel.) Ronald E. Schira Collection

**David R. Francis
President of the
Lousiana Purchase
Exposition Company**

After several years of preparation, a group of energetic businessmen led by David R. Francis, the dynamic president of the Exposition Company, put the plan into motion. At the turn of the twentieth century, St. Louis was the fourth largest city in the United States, and fair organizers knew that a fair would further encourage development. With the motto "Nothing Impossible," they planned an incredible celebration that put St. Louis on the map. In March 1901, Congress passed legislation that endorsed the fair and approved a start-up funding proposal — $5 million appropriated from the federal government to follow $5 million from the city coffers through the sale of municipal bonds, and $5 million to be raised by selling stock in the fair to the citizens of St. Louis. By coincidence, the monies raised to initiate the effort to commemorate the Louisiana Purchase equaled the cost of the entire Louisiana Territory.

Map of the fairgrounds relative to Forest Park

President William McKinley invited the nations of the world to participate in the upcoming exposition with a proclamation that stated, "I do hereby invite all the nations of the earth to take part in the commemoration . . . by appointing representatives and sending such exhibits to the Louisiana Purchase Exposition as will most fitly and fully illustrate their resources, their industries and their progress in civilization. " The theme of the fair was education — at every level. This was a marked departure from other fairs because the Louisiana Purchase Exposition was not to be just a display of products, but an international university. Numerous exhibitors signed up to not only show their wares, but the processes underlying them.

Many conferences, called congresses in those days, were scheduled to gather authorities in all fields to share their ideas, experiences, and research results. With the plans and funding in place, building construction commenced with groundbreaking in December 1901.

Illinois Building under construction

The site chosen for the fair was a large tract of land with low hills and a small lake on the western end of the city's Forest Park. When the 657-acre section of wild parkland proved insufficient to accommodate the growing needs of the fair, the Exposition Company leased the campus and the newly constructed buildings of Washington University, adjacent to the fairgrounds. Additional property to the south of the university was also obtained, resulting in 1,272 acres devoted to the exposition, the largest ever. The land was cleared while the crooked River Des Peres that snaked through the fairgrounds was channeled and covered. Thousands of workmen transformed the wooded parkland into a breathtaking kingdom.

Construction of the 1,576 fair buildings and structures was a monumental effort. Tradesmen and construction workers created a city of fleeting beauty, but with all the infrastructure and services required to meet the daily needs of visitors.

The large exhibit palaces alone were massive undertakings, each covering acres of space. All were framed of long-leaf yellow pine; an estimated ninety million linear feet were used. The exteriors of the main palaces were constructed of an ivory-tinted material called "staff." Staff was a mixture of plaster of paris, water, and hemp as a binder that could be molded into intricate designs. It was an inexpensive material, yet durable for short-term use. It could be quickly made and was effective in creating a wonderland of buildings in the elaborately decorative Beaux Arts style. Twelve hundred allegorical and historical statues, also created from staff, depicted themes of western expansion throughout the fairgrounds. Most of the states and territories erected buildings to welcome and entertain visitors, as did foreign nations from all corners of the world.

(Francis) Ronald E. Schira Collection

David R. Francis presses the telegraph key to signal the opening of the 1904 World's Fair

As 1903 drew near, fair organizers knew that the exposition would not be ready and sought a postponement for one year. As a result, David R. Francis and the Exposition Company worked tirelessly to attract additional exhibitors. By opening day in 1904, fifty-three foreign nations, forty-three states, several territories, and a multitude of businesses had products, exhibits, and demonstrations under way or in place for fair visitors.

On April 30, 1904, Fair President Francis had the honor of opening the long-awaited festivities. At the ceremonies he eloquently proclaimed, "Open ye gates! Swing wide ye portals! Enter herein ye sons of men! Learn the lesson here taught and gather from it inspiration for still greater accomplishments!" Pressing a telegraph key shortly after one o'clock in the afternoon, he notified President Theodore Roosevelt to press a key at the White House in return. With that, the fair came alive as flags unfurled and fountains surged forth to herald the start of the largest event ever staged by the city of St. Louis. John Philip Sousa's band played for the celebration and a 500-person choir sang "Hymn of the West," the official song of the fair.

Fairgoers flocked to St. Louis in the ensuing months — nearly twenty million when the final counts were tabulated. For those with time to spend, there was ample time to see the sights. The fairgrounds operated from 8:00 a.m. to 11:30 p.m., Monday through Saturday. The exhibit palaces opened at 9:00 a.m. and closed at dusk, but the entertainment midway called the Pike beckoned visitors both day and night.

At fifty cents for adults and twenty-five cents for children, an unforget-table world of knowledge, fascina-tion, and fun awaited visitors just beyond the turnstiles.

Described as the "Main Picture," Festival Hall and the Cascades formed the panoramic focal point that greeted visitors entering the fairgrounds through the main gate.

(Bennitt) Author

The Main Picture — Festival Hall and the Cascades

This spectacular centerpiece was located on the terrace above the Grand Basin. Festival Hall dominated the view and served as a music auditorium that housed the world's largest organ. Audiences were entertained by numerous concerts during the fair. The gold-leafed dome of Festival Hall was larger than Saint Peter's in Rome. Two pavilions, the "Atlantic" and the "Pacific," flanked the Hall, symbolically representing the expanse of the nation. Each pavilion contained a restaurant. Water flowed down the stepped terraces below Festival Hall and its twin pavilions into the Grand Basin. At night, colored lights illuminated the cascades for a spectacular visual effect.

Eight large exhibit palaces radiated from Festival Hall in a fan-like arrangement around the Grand Basin and lagoons. The decorative buildings and water features, accented by bridges and statuary of all types, offered the fairgoer dreamlike vistas. Most of the seventy thousand fair exhibits were located in these palaces that showcased the latest innovations and products from all corners of the world.

Palace of Electricity

One palace was devoted to the emerging electrical age that would transform lifestyles in the twentieth century. The Palace of Electricity demonstrated how electricity had been harnessed for the benefit of man by featuring wireless telegraph and telephone communication, electric heating and cooking, and light bulbs of every size and color. The humble, but now indispensable, electrical plug and wall outlet were introduced to the world in 1904. Thomas Edison, the famous inventor, oversaw the exhibits in the palace, including his latest innovations. At night the fairgrounds were aglow. Incandescent bulbs were lavishly used to outline the buildings and to illuminate the grand vistas to the delight of visitors.

The Palace of Manufactures, the equivalent of an international shopping center, featured products of nine hundred industries. Japan, Germany, and France led all others with extensive exhibits. The latest styles of fabrics, carpets, glass, crystal, shoes, and hats were among the items viewed and purchased by fairgoers. Furniture, hardware, and home decor filled the aisles. With the continuing perfection of the manufacturing process, shoppers found items once considered luxuries now affordable.

Palace of Manufactures

**Palace of Education and
Social Economy**

The Palace of Education and Social Economy was an experience in knowledge from kindergarten to the university level. It was the embodiment of the educational theme of the fair — and the first time that an entire fair building was dedicated exclusively for that purpose. Demonstration classrooms showed the latest teaching techniques. Many schools and colleges provided exhibits, including those that instructed students with hearing and speech impairments.

The Palace of Varied Industries exhibited artistic pottery and glass, furniture, and jewelry. Again Germany and Japan brought the largest displays of items created by their skilled craftspeople.

Palace of Varied Industries

The Palace of Mines and Metallurgy, with its distinctive entrances flanked by Egyptian obelisks, showed the mineral resources of the world and the machines involved in processing them. Steel manufacturing, foundry work, well drilling, and precious metal mining were all demonstrated within the nine-acre building and at related sites on the fairgrounds. The palace contained an array of exhibits. Natural spring waters were included, with displays from one hundred and fifty bottlers across the country. The state of Louisiana displayed a statue of Lot's wife in salt. In a small, darkened room, visitors could view experiments showing the unusual properties of the element radium.

Palace of Mines and Metallurgy

The Palace of Transportation, identified by its great archways, exhibited all the methods that man had either used or invented to travel — from animals to the world's largest locomotives. Four miles of track in the building displayed historical trains, as well as the latest innovations in rail travel. Many visitors were keenly interested in the mode of transportation recently introduced on American roadways — the automobile. The early autos experimented with all types of fuel: some ran on gas, some were electric, and others used steam. The "showrooms" at the fair featured 140 models.

Palace of Transportation and showroom

The Palace of Liberal Arts amazed visitors with its sixty-thousand-seat auditorium, newly invented X-ray machines, and the latest in printing presses. Other impressive displays included a large collection of musical instruments; carvings; temple adornments and weapons from China; model lighthouses; photography exhibits; and typewriters. The fair's Daily Official Program for September 15, 1904, included this item:

Palace of Liberal Arts

ELECTRIC TYPEWRITERS
A special display of the operation of Electric Typewriters takes place to-day in the Blickensderfer Booth, Block 23, Palace of Liberal Arts. The machine is entirely novel and represents a distinct departure in the development of the typewriter. The demonstrations take place daily and continuously till 6 p.m. A machine will be given away to the lucky guesser of attendance. Guess cards at the Blickensderfer Booth.

Palace of Machinery

The Palace of Machinery featured powerful engines, turbines, generators, and pumps — true products of the Industrial Age. It also housed the power plant for the fair that generated 45,000 horsepower (about 33 thousand kilowatts). The impressive building could always be identified by its six tall towers.

The Art Palace was directly behind Festival Hall. Although built on a smaller scale than the other great exhibit halls, it was constructed of fireproof materials, insurance for the great artwork displayed within. The building was constructed of limestone and brick. Two temporary wings, also built of brick, and an international sculpture pavilion with adjoining gardens completed the art complex. The central section of the Art Palace was erected as a permanent structure to be retained after the fair. It would provide spacious quarters for a new art museum to replace the old downtown facility known as the St. Louis Museum of Fine Arts that was under the direction of Washington University.

Palace of Art

Three other palaces, devoted to the cultivation of plants, farming, and forestry, occupied space in the farther reaches of the fairgrounds.

The Palace of Agriculture was the largest of all. It covered an area of twenty acres. Similar to the displays at state fairs, many farm products were exhibited, some in the most creative ways. An elephant made of almonds, a bear of prunes, and life-size butter sculptures of all types grabbed the visitors' attention. Within the palace, several states built pavilions elaborately decorated with corn and wheat. Farm equipment companies and food processing firms erected attractive booths to advertise their products. Just outside, the giant floral clock kept time on the adjacent terrace.

Palace of Agriculture

Palace of Horticulture

The Palace of Horticulture, constructed in the shape of a Greek cross, had two main wings. The central section contained extensive displays of fruit, nuts, and melons. On certain days, visitors gladly accepted free samples of apples and other fruit. Fifty thousand peaches were given away on August 15 to celebrate "Missouri Peach Day." The glass-enclosed East Wing served as a conservatory for floral shows and tropical plant exhibits. The West Wing displayed cut flowers, horticultural implements, and beekeeping methods.

Livestock barns and pens filled the southwest corner of the fairgrounds behind the Horticulture Palace. Prizes were awarded in all categories of competition from pigeons to the largest draft horses.

The Palace of Forestry, Fish and Game was the smallest of the major exhibit palaces, yet it included a wide variety of nature displays. Visitors viewed fish of all types in numerous aquariums, as well as freshwater and saltwater pools. The palace also devoted space to wild game and forestry exhibits.

Palace of Forestry, Fish and Game

The United States Government had extensive displays representing all branches of government. The United States Mint demonstrated the coining process, but produced medals instead of coins for distribution to the visitors. All types of guns and artillery were exhibited inside the building and in outdoor embankments. The Life-Saving Service attracted large crowds to its daily drill. Stamps and currency production were featured by the Treasury Department. West Point cadets and Marines trained and paraded at the fair. The Smithsonian Institution and National Museum brought archaeological, biological, and anthropological exhibits, including a reproduction of a Stegosaurus dinosaur.

Fifty-three foreign nations participated in the fair, and many of them erected buildings to represent the architectural styles

Philippine Village

found in their countries. France built a replica of the Grand Trianon of Versailles with its opulent interior. Germany reproduced the Charlottenberg Castle with its palatial rooms. Great Britain copied the brick and stone Orangery at Kensington Palace. Italy reproduced a Roman emperor's villa. China duplicated Prince Pu Lun's summer residence, while Austria's "secession" styled building — with an interior decorated with art nouveau motifs — was the latest in European architectural design.

As the result of the Spanish-American War, the United States received the Philippine Islands as a protectorate. To give fair visitors a glimpse of Filipino culture and life, the fair fathers organized an extensive exhibit covering forty-seven acres. Members of several tribal groups

Still Shining

were brought to the fair and constructed small villages in their native style. The Philippine exhibit attracted the curiosity of many who had never encountered remote cultures.

The Philippine village was the largest of the numerous "exhibits" of the Department of Anthropology. The focus of this department was man's study of man rather than his products. Native peoples from all inhabited continents were brought to the fair as part of this cultural study. The methods used and conclusions drawn reflected the theories of a bygone era that have long since been transcended.

(Francis) Ronald E. Schira Collection

Washington State Pavilion

At the time of the fair, forty-five states comprised the nation. Most of the states, as well as the Alaska, Arizona, New Mexico, Oklahoma, and Indian territories, constructed pavilions to promote their industries and to welcome visitors. Many of these pavilions were reproductions of historic buildings. Others were composites of prominent structures in the state or totally unique designs. Tennessee displayed Andrew Jackson's home, the Hermitage. Louisiana reproduced the Cabildo, the site of the signing of transfer papers for the lower Louisiana Territory. A copy of "Beauvoir," the last home of Jefferson Davis, was Mississippi's contribution. Virginia entertained visitors at a replica of Thomas Jefferson's Monticello. South Dakota's entry resembled an old Spanish mission, while Iowa combined the architecture of the old and new capitol buildings in Iowa City and Des Moines. Texas' unique design was based on a five-pointed "lone" star, and the state of Washington erected a cone-shaped building, "The Wigwam," made completely of native woods. The state houses received out-of-towners by providing space for receptions and relaxation.

The fair was an international university, not only educating the casual visitor, but by inviting leading authorities in all of the academic disciplines to share their knowledge in the International Congresses. Experts in the arts and sciences, agriculture and commerce, as well as journalists and lawyers, attended to discuss the latest advancements in research and scholarly thought. In the political realm, the Democratic Party selected St. Louis as the site for its national convention and nominated Alton B. Parker and Henry G. Davis as the ticket for the November elections. Many of the attendees caucused and conferred at the Washington University facilities.

Camel rides

All types of conveyances moved fairgoers throughout the extensive grounds. The main method of travel was the intramural railroad that was actually a streetcar with seventeen stops near fair attractions. In addition, there were roller chairs and jinrickshaws; swan boats, serpent boats and gondolas; automobiles; miniature trains; and even burros, camels, and giant turtles — all for a memorable ride.

The Giant Observation Wheel afforded the best view of the fair. At twenty-five stories high, it was one of the grandest attractions. For fifty cents, those who dared went two revolutions in one of the thirty-six cars that held sixty people each. There were reports of a dinner party within one of the spacious cars, a daredevil who rode on the roof, and even a couple seated on ponies who exchanged wedding vows as their car reached the highest point.

Giant Observation Wheel

The Pike, a mile-long midway at the fair, was a favorite day and night. When the palaces closed each evening, fairgoers migrated to the Pike as barkers competed with enticements for those seeking to be amused. Wonderful rides called Creation, the Hereafter, the Magic Whirlpool, New York to the North Pole, and Under and Over the Sea thrilled those who paid the fare. There were shows, too. The Battle of Santiago was staged on a small lake with its miniature ships engaged in a fiery battle; the Galveston Flood recounted that 1900 event with a sea of storms; and the Japanese Spider Dance concluded with a web that entangled the entire stage. The Temple of Mirth was a fun house that amused all, especially with its maze of mirrors that distorted reflections. Hagenbeck's Wild Animal Circus, an ostrich farm, and exotic bazaars fascinated visitors. The Pike was a cornucopia of sights and sounds for wide-eyed visitors bent on having a good time.

Louisiana Purchase Exposition St. Louis 1904
The Pike looking East from Streets of Cairo

The Pike

Still Shining

Lore has it that food vendors on the Pike created three American favorites: the ice cream cone, iced tea, and the hot dog. Although it is more likely that these items were popularized at the fair, each generated its own legend. Reportedly, an ice cream vendor, short on plates, creatively used a neighboring concessionaire's waffles to solve his dilemma. Rolling the waffles into cones, he added scoops of ice cream and created a tasty treat. The hot tea salesman had few patrons on the warm summer days until he poured his drink over crushed ice. And the sausage vendor wrapped his links in bakery buns and called them "hot dogs."

In conjunction with the fair, St. Louis also hosted the 1904 Olympics on the fairgrounds. These Olympic Games were the first ever held in the United States. Competitors entered on an individual basis and without qualifying trials. Many athletes represented clubs from various cities and universities. Although most of the participants were American, there were a number of foreign competitors. Despite the fact that there were many unofficial Olympic contests at the fair, thirteen Olympic records were set in the twenty-two official events that were held.

1904 Olympic Games

After seven fabulous months, thousands of St. Louisans gathered on December 1, 1904, for the official closing of the event that had captivated the city. The day was dedicated to Exposition President David R. Francis, the man who brilliantly led the effort to plan, organize, build, and operate the fair. He worked tirelessly in turning his vision into a reality that now no one wanted to forget. As midnight drew near, President Francis took one last look at the splendid view. With a heavy heart, he delivered the final proclamation and closed the fair amidst music and fireworks for one last farewell.

Closing night fireworks in the image of David R. Francis

The fabulous fair was over, but its endearing memories lived on in the spirit and minds of countless St. Louisans. Special mementos from those glory days have been treasured by numerous families and handed down as cherished heirlooms. Many share a special connection to that magical time through family lore or just fascination with the fleeting kingdom that once welcomed the world to St. Louis.

Buildings and Structures

Many of the State pavilions have already been disposed of, some to remain in and near St. Louis, others to be sent to the State they represent, while others will be used as summer homes in various parts of the United States, having been purchased for that purpose by individuals. Wrecking companies have bought a few of the buildings for the material they contain, and most of those now unsold probably will be sold for wreckage.

St. Louis Republic
December 4, 1904

White Hall – Connecticut State Pavilion

The state of Connecticut's contribution to the fair was a replica of an elegant country house known as the Sigourney mansion built in Hartford during the early 1800s. The façade of the structure combined both Roman and Greek styling and was highlighted by an impressive portico supported by four large columns. The interior design recreated architectural features popular in some of the finest colonial homes in Connecticut, including an oval-shaped balcony on the second floor crowning the open well above the center hallway on the floor below.

Connecticut Pavilion exterior

The first floor served as a museum, showcasing historical furnishings and artwork lent by Connecticut families and artists. A chair transported on the Mayflower, George Washington's desk from the Continental Congress, and furniture created for Marie Antoinette were displayed in the collection.

Built at a cost of $31,000, the house was sold by bid for an undisclosed price at the close of the fair. It was resold to Indiana businessman, William S. Potter, who was originally outbid — much to his wife's disappointment.

Connecticut Pavilion interior

The Potters had the structure dismantled and moved the numbered pieces by rail for reassembly in Lafayette, Indiana. There the building was reconstructed and faithfully restored to the original design in accordance with an agreement with the Connecticut Commission to the fair. Rebuilt on a five-acre tract in Lafayette, it was nicknamed "White Hall," although the white plaster exterior was replaced with buff-colored brick walls. The Potters hired an architect to modify the interior for residential living; a kitchen and a breakfast room were added. Administrative offices were converted to bedrooms and activity rooms. Later, an addition was made to the second story, but the front elevation of the building essentially reflects the original 1904 appearance.

In 1984, the home was sold. The new owners worked to return the stately mansion to its turn-of-the-century splendor through exterior renovations and period redecorating. Highlights include museum-quality oil paintings from Indiana's most acclaimed impressionist artists known as the Hoosier Group. One of the pieces by William Forsyth titled *Cliff Road* was originally displayed in the Indiana Pavilion at the fair. With twenty-two rooms, the home provides ten thousand square feet of living space.

The restored Connecticut House is a splendid example of an original state pavilion and stands as a true legacy to the St. Louis Fair.

Haan-Potter Home (1904 Connecticut Pavilion)
Lafayette, Indiana

Warm and Wonderful – The American Radiator Building

The American Radiator Company of Chicago advertised its innovative hot water heating system in a full-scale model home at the fair. The two-story house was erected inside the spacious Palace of Manufactures.

Visitors interested in hot water heating systems could view the compact boiler unit, steam pipe connections, and location of the radiators in a cutaway model that was without its front walls. The house was fully decorated to show how radiators could harmonize with the furnishings. The complete display represented a home with a cost of about $5,000. More than eighty thousand fairgoers had registered at the exhibit by the end of July 1904.

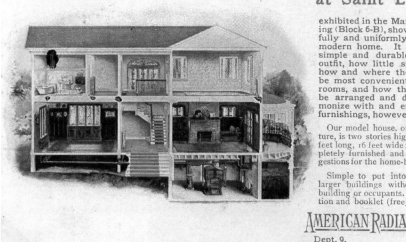

IDEAL Boilers — AMERICAN Radiators

Souvenir card from the model house

As described by Mark Bennitt in the *History of the Louisiana Purchase Exposition*, the exhibitor took the functional radiator to artistic heights to appeal to the decorative interests of the homemaker:

> The "American" radiators are so choicely modeled and moulded, so carefully finished in detail, that when decorated they very much assist to furnish the rooms in which they are placed. They are made in about thirty-six plain, semi-ornate and extra artistic designs and in many different shapes, for narrow and contracted spaces, for corners, bay window seats, side walls, etc.

32

After the fair, the colonial-styled structure was sold at auction. It was moved by rail to Webster Groves, Missouri, where it was reconstructed at its present location on Kenilworth Place. The partial house was made whole with an extension constructed on the front to enclose the cutaway and with the addition of a kitchen. The leaded glass windows and much of the original woodwork were reinstalled. A stucco finish was applied to the frame exterior. Other renovations and updates have transformed the former fair exhibit into a handsome and spacious residence.

American Radiator Building today
Webster Groves, Missouri

Permanent — The Palace of Art

The Board of Directors of the Louisiana Purchase Exposition had determined that there would be one lasting gift to the city of St. Louis at the close of the fair. That gift would be an art museum, or as Exposition President David R. Francis stated, "the one material monument." A monumental museum, the fair's most outstanding legacy, was built as a gift that continues to give.

Palace of Art

The fair planners engaged noted architect Cass Gilbert to design a fireproof structure to safely display irreplaceable works of art. Of the 1,576 buildings erected at the fair, the Palace of Art was the only one constructed of permanent materials for long-term use. Largely built of Bedford gray limestone and buff-colored Roman brick, it is accented with a limited use of bronze and marble. Of Roman-Classical design with Corinthian colonnades, it was erected on Art Hill behind the showy focal point of the fair, Festival Hall and the Cascade Terraces. The main museum building was flanked by two temporary wings (constructed of brick with staff decorations). A structure to the rear of the palace served as the international sculpture pavilion. The Grand Court of the main building featured a 78-foot-high vaulted ceiling and numerous free standing and relief sculptures by accomplished American artists. A maze of 134 sky-lit galleries was accessible from the main hall, all on one single level. Six symbolic figures were installed over the front portico to recall the great periods of art: Egyptian, Classic, Gothic, Oriental, Renaissance, and Modern. Medallions on the façade of the building honored the great artists of the world.

The collection of sculpture and artwork at the fair was notable. Rather than limiting displays to historical art as was done at previous fairs, St. Louis emphasized the contemporary work of living artists with the classical. There were six general classifications of art: painting; sculpture; etchings, engravings and autolithographics; architecture; industrial and functional art; as well as selected works from public and private collections.

**The St. Louis Art Museum
St. Louis, Missouri**

Artwork was purposefully arranged in the palace with central focus on the American pieces and artists — and foreign influence upon them. The Grand Court and galleries in the central building were devoted exclusively to art and sculpture executed by American artists trained in the United States. Beyond those galleries were the works of Americans who studied art abroad. Rooms in the farthest reaches of the museum featured the art of foreign artists who have been the source of inspiration for many Americans. The visitor was challenged to view American achievements in art within this stratified context.

Two large allegorical figures personifying painting and sculpture were seated on either side of the staircase at the main entrance to the Art Palace. Each had been formed in staff for the fair. *Painting* was the creation of Louis St.-Gaudens and *Sculpture* was accomplished by Daniel Chester French, who had other significant works on exhibit just inside the museum. In 1913, both of the larger-than-life symbolic figures were recreated in marble for permanent installation in front of the museum.

***Sculpture*
Daniel Chester French**

The equestrian statue of St. Louis' patron and namesake, Louis IX, also traces its origins to the fair. Now astride Art Hill directly in front of the Art Museum, the sculpture by Charles H. Niehaus, cast in bronze in 1906, was originally created in staff for the fair and titled the *Apotheosis of St. Louis*. The inscription on the base of the permanent statue reads

***Painting*
Louis St.-Gaudens**

"Presented to the City of St. Louis by the Louisiana Purchase Exposition Company in commemoration of the Universal Exposition of 1904 held on this site."

Three years after the fair and at the decision of city voters, the Art Museum became the first tax-supported museum in the country. With public ownership and the legacy of free admission from the fair, no entry fee has ever been charged, still true to the inscription above the entrance that states, "Dedicated to Art and Free to All."

The Louisiana Exhibition 1904, St. Louis, Mo. Statue of St. Louis

Apotheosis of St. Louis
1904 World's Fair

A view of *St. Louis* by Charles Niehaus today

Wee Bungalow – Nevada State Pavilion

Smaller by comparison to other state buildings, Nevada's hospitality house at the 1904 World's Fair was dubbed with the nickname "Wee Bungalow." A porch and second-story veranda spanned the full length of the structure to provide added sitting space for weary guests. Construction costs for the cozy pavilion were $5,200.

Nevada's early fame and fortune followed the discovery of gold and silver in the Comstock Lode in 1859. That heritage spawned the state's mining industry that was amply displayed in pictures and specimens at the fair. Gold, silver, copper, lead, and precious stones from Nevada's mines awed visitors at the state's exhibit in the Palace of Mines and Metallurgy.

The state house was erected to overlook The Gulch with its working mines, derricks, and smelters. In The Gulch, Nevada introduced the world to Borax Bill. Each day, Bill drove his twenty-mule team and wagons laden with borax mined in the Nevada desert through the gap to the delight of fairgoers.

The Nevada Pavilion escaped the wrecking crews when the fair closed. It was dismantled and sent by rail for reconstruction as a residential home. With extensive alterations, the house was rebuilt on Schultz Road in the community of Oakland, a suburb of St. Louis.

(Francis) Ronald E. Schira Collection

**Nevada Pavilion
1904 World's Fair**

Photo by Author

**Nevada Pavilion today
Oakland, Missouri**

(Bayne) Ronald E. Schira Collection

Borax Bill's twenty-mule team, 1904 World's Fair

Frontier Justice – Cahokia Courthouse

Photo by Author

Restored Cahokia Courthouse
Cahokia, Illinois

Among the elaborate Beaux Arts palaces and stately pavilions at the fair was a historic structure that recalled, to some degree, the French-colonial heritage of the Mississippi Valley. Perhaps the oldest public building in the Midwest, the reconstructed Cahokia Courthouse, from the nearby Illinois town of the same name, actually gave visitors a distorted glimpse of French-colonial architecture. Yet it also bore an authentic connection to the Lewis and Clark expedition.

The building had a colorful past before it was moved across the mighty Mississippi to serve as a curiosity on the fairgrounds. The original building was constructed about 1737 for the Saucier family in the village of Cahokia. It was built using walnut timbers in the French style known as poteaux-sur-solle (post-on-sill). A stone foundation, two feet thick, supported a log sill along which additional logs were aligned vertically. The uprights were chinked with rock and mortar to form the walls. The roof line was pitched and extended beyond the structure to create a veranda on all sides.

In 1793, the building was purchased by court officials of St. Clair County; it served as a courthouse for the Northwest Territory until 1800. It continued to be the judicial center during territorial reorganizations, serving the Indiana Territory from 1801 to 1809. In 1801, the boundaries of the country were so extensive that the frontier court held jurisdiction to the Canadian border. During the winter of preparation before the exploration of the Louisiana Territory, Meriwether Lewis visited the Cahokia Courthouse, which also served as a post office, to correspond with President Jefferson. The Illinois Territory utilized the courthouse from 1809 until 1814, when the county seat was moved to the growing settlement of Belleville. The building was used during the remainder of the century as a residence, town hall, warehouse, and even operated for a time as a saloon.

Flood waters took their toll on the Cahokia Courthouse many times. By 1900, the building had deteriorated to the extent that it was only used for storage. In 1901, the dilapidated building was sold at auction to East St. Louis businessman, Alexander Cella, and dismantled. He stored the old timbers on his property until he recognized an opportunity to use the building as a money-making concession at the St. Louis World's Fair. The building was reconstructed on the edge of the Plateau of States, just to the east of the Art Palace. At the fairgrounds, the refashioned courthouse was a fraction of its original size and only hinted at the original design. It was reduced from four rooms to just one room. The logs were positioned upright and close together without the chinking. It was reported that the leftover timbers were cut into wooden cigars and sold as souvenirs. Cella was unable to obtain a permit to sell beer at the building, so the exhibit included documents, benches, a table, and a gavel, all reminiscent of the structure's legal past.

Location of Cahokia Courthouse on the fairgrounds (upper left)

Modified Cahokia Courthouse — similar to its appearance on the fairgrounds

At the close of the fair, the building was once again dismantled and sold. Purchased for the Chicago Historical Society and the Chicago Centennial Commission, it was returned to Illinois, but reconstructed in Jackson Park in Chicago. Cahokians were appalled and demanded to have the courthouse sent back to its original site. After years of negotiating the return, with plans for a full restoration based on archaeological and historical research, the courthouse was shipped back to Cahokia in 1939. The building was carefully reconstructed to the original design, incorporating as many of the old logs as possible. In 1940, the restored building was dedicated and remains a splendid remnant of the French-colonial heritage of the Mississippi Valley.

Under the Domes — West Virginia State Pavilion

The Louisiana Exhibition 1904
St. Louis, Mo.
West-Virginia

West Virginia Pavilion

"The first floor is occupied chiefly by an immense hall, with very high ceilings, of ornamental metal donated by manufacturers in the State."

Louisiana and the Fair, Volume VI, J.W. Buel

Restoration and research support neighborhood lore that decorative features of the West Virginia Pavilion were incorporated in the large Greek Revival home on East Monroe Avenue in Oakland, a St. Louis suburb. Completed in 1906, the semicircular porch that dominates the front of the house today reused columns and portions of a dome salvaged from the fair building. The interior of the house is highlighted with other embellishments from the West Virginia Pavilion, most noteworthy are the ornate pressed-metal ceiling panels found in every downstairs room.

Interior of the pavilion

The ivory-white West Virginia Building was reminiscent of a county seat or state capitol building. It was an imposing structure, colonial in design, topped with four classic Greek domes at the corners of the roof, and a larger dome in the center. Spacious porches on three sides of the building welcomed visitors to explore its museum, climb to the center dome observatory for a grand view, or attend events in the reception and banquet halls.

A description of the interior in Mark Bennitt's *History of the Louisiana Purchase Exposition* also noted, "Throughout the building were ornamental metallic ceilings."

West Virginia Building today
Oakland, Missouri

The December 4, 1904, edition of the *St. Louis Republic* stated that "The West Virginia building has also been sold to a wrecking company for $800, the original cost being $22,300. The furnishings will be distributed to different State institutions."

Records show that after the fair, portions of the West Virginia Building were sent for use in the construction of a home at the East Monroe address.

Pressed-metal ceiling detail

Spreading the Word — The Press Building

The first structure completed on the fairgrounds was the World's Fair Press Building. It was dedicated on October 25, 1902, ready to welcome thousands of newspaper correspondents and journalists from all over the world. The building had already been pressed into service at two previous expositions to promote the upcoming St. Louis fair. Constructed in Buffalo, New York, it was the Louisiana Purchase Exposition Building for the 1901 Pan-American Exposition. It was moved to Charleston for the South Carolina Interstate and West Indian Exposition in 1902 to again advertise the 1904 fair.

When reconstructed on the St. Louis fairgrounds, the building was a two-story structure with spacious verandas on three sides. Gala receptions were held inside the first-floor lounging rooms that could seat two hundred people. Eleven apartments accommodated long-term guests.

The Press Building

AMATEUR PRESS CONGRESS AT THE WORLD'S FAIR, ST. LOUIS.
AMATEUR JOURNALISTS' DAY, JULY 2, 1904.

Amateur Journalists' Day at the Fair (left)

Official Press Pass (right)

Still Shining

At the close of the fair, the wooden building was sold and partially rebuilt as a residence at its present site on Clark Avenue in Webster Groves, Missouri. In its redesign, the house is now approximately two-thirds of its original size. The verandas were removed, but the roof lines and dormer reflect the homestead style of the original structure. Interior modifications in later years included an extensive remodeling of the original kitchen.

Photo by Yvonne Suess

The Press Building today
Webster Groves, Missouri

Older than Oklahoma – Oklahoma Territory Pavilion

In 1904, the United States boasted forty-five states within its borders. Looking toward statehood, the Oklahoma Territory erected a building of Spanish and Moorish design on the Plateau of States. Workmen applied Oklahoma cement to create the stucco exterior and capped the building with a red tile roof. Expansive verandas with pillared archways decorated the façade of the building and provided shaded comfort for visitors and guests. The interior was designed for hospitality; the first floor had a reception area and two parlors. The second floor contained displays of art and Oklahoma history.

"Oklahoma Day" was celebrated on September 6, 1904. It was a full day of celebration. The planned events, listed in the August 19, 1904, edition of the *El Reno Globe,* included speeches, music, a parade, informal reception, and "free watermelon" to be "served to the entire world on the lawn of the Oklahoma Building." In his *Universal Exposition of 1904,* David R. Francis describes the event: "Two thousand of these melons, each weighing from fifty to one hundred pounds, were cut open by waiters and served to visitors, regardless of the section of the country from which they came."

After the fair, the building was acquired by the El Reno Oklahoma Elks Lodge #743 as the permanent home for that newly founded organization. The stucco

Oklahoma Territory Pavilion

Oklahoma Pavilion interior

Still Shining

exterior was cut into sections and the framing was taken apart. The dismantled building was stacked on flatbed rail cars, transported to Oklahoma, and re-erected at a cost of $11,250. Dedication services were held on November 20, 1905, less than a year after the fair closed.

Over the years, the building has been remodeled and modernized to preserve it for continuous use. A band shell was added in 1915. After World War II, the porches were enclosed to expand the interior space. Kitchen facilities have been updated and the well-used ballroom floor was replaced for the third time.

Photo by Yvonne Suess

The building has always been a haven for hospitality. Fair visitors in St. Louis could relax, write a note to a friend, or catch up on Oklahoma news from the file of territorial newspapers. During World War II, the lodge building served as a fraternal center for thousands of soldiers stationed at military installations in the vicinity or who traveled through El Reno on troop trains or in highway transports.

The lodge continues to serve the community today by extending its services and building space for conventions, civic functions, and youth activities.

El Reno Oklahoma Elks Lodge #743
El Reno, Oklahoma

Hardscrabble – General Grant's Cabin

At the 1904 fair, the C. F. Blanke Coffee Company paid tribute to America's eighteenth president, Ulysses S. Grant, by exhibiting the log home that Grant had built by hand some fifty years earlier as a farmer in the St. Louis area.

In 1854, after resigning from an eleven-year military career, Captain Grant moved to St. Louis to be reunited with his wife, Julia Dent Grant, and family. As a gift from her father, Julia had received about one hundred acres of land near the Dent's family home at White Haven, in the wilderness of St. Louis County. Here the Grants planned to raise their family and farm the land.

In the autumn of 1855, Grant began preparations for building his now famous cabin. Grant cut and notched timbers from local oak and elm trees. In 1856, he enlisted the aid of neighbors for the house raising, but completed the roof, flooring, and stairs himself. A marker in Saint Paul's Churchyard on South Rock Hill Road in St. Louis County identifies the original location that Grant chose for his home.

Most accounts indicate that the house had four rooms — two upstairs and two downstairs, with a center hallway on each floor. It was a rugged frontier home, appropriately named Hardscrabble. The Grants lived in the cabin only three or four months. Upon the death of Julia's mother, the family moved to nearby White Haven.

Unsuccessful at farming, Grant pursued other ventures prior to his rise to national prominence after the outbreak of the Civil War. He retained the cabin, however, until 1884 when financial difficulties resulted in a transfer of ownership to William

GENERAL FRED D. GRANT at the cabin built by his father GEN. U.S. GRANT IN 1854. St. Louis Worlds Fair 1904. Now owned by C.F. BLANKE.

A postcard depicting Gen. Fred D. Grant (son of Ulysses S. Grant) in front of Grant's Cabin (left)

Grant's Cabin reconstructed at the 1904 World's Fair (right)

Vanderbilt of New York. Luther Conn subsequently purchased the farm and cabin. In 1891, the cabin was sold to Edward Joy, who moved it to Old Orchard (Webster Groves, Missouri) to be used to promote his real estate business. In 1903, the home was sold, dismantled, and moved again. It was reconstructed at the 1904 St. Louis World's Fair and opened as a public attraction and lunch concession by the C. F. Blanke Coffee Company. Fair visitors could see the cabin in its wooded site near the east wing of the Art Palace.

(Postcard: #1078, V.O. Hammon Pub. Co.) Author

Grant's Cabin after the fair

Sometime after the fair, Adolphus Busch bought the cabin and had it reconstructed on the grounds of his estate in 1907. Part of the Busch property included the land of General Grant's old farm, and in honor of the general, Busch named his estate Grant's Farm. For years, travelers on Gravois Road in the south St. Louis County community of Affton have viewed the old cabin beyond the fence wrought from over two thousand Civil War rifle barrels.

In 1977, the structure underwent a complete restoration. It was dismantled a fourth time and the deteriorating sections of the structure were replaced. Anheuser-Busch restored both the interior and exterior of the building to its 1850's appearance.

Today the cabin not only stands as a legacy of our eighteenth president, but also as a well-preserved remnant of the 1904 World's Fair.

Photo by Nancy Schuster

**Grant's Cabin today
Busch Estate, St. Louis County**

Photos by Yvonne Suess

THIS TABLET MARKS THE ORIGINAL SITE OF "HARDSCRABBLE" LOG CABIN HOME BUILT BY ULYSSES S. GRANT IN 1854.
ERECTED BY THE
WEBSTER GROVES CHAPTER
DAUGHTERS OF THE AMERICAN REVOLUTION
1946

**Marker identifying original site of Grant's Cabin
St. Paul's Churchyard, St. Louis County**

For the Birds — 1904 Flight Cage

Flight Cage, 1904

Ronald E. Schira Collection

One of the premiere treasures of St. Louis is the magnificent Flight Cage at the St. Louis Zoo. The Smithsonian Institution erected this walk-through aviary at the Louisiana Purchase Exposition as part of the United States Government exhibit.

The mammoth structure was designed for free-flight of both exotic and native birds, much to the delight of fairgoers. Designed to educate visitors, a large collection of birds indigenous to the United States could be observed in the giant display. The cage was constructed of steel ribs and wire mesh on a wooden base by the St. Paul Foundry Company. It was built at a cost of $17,500.

Covered walkway

St. Louis Zoological Board of Control, Author

Interior of Flight Cage, 1904

(Rau) Author

With impressive dimensions of 228 feet long, 84 feet wide, and 50 feet high, it was the largest bird cage ever constructed. A screen-covered walkway (or arcade) extended the entire length of the cage and invited visitors to view the birds from within their habitat. The aviary was partitioned lengthwise; larger birds such as geese, pelicans, and cranes squawked in the northern section, while smaller birds such as canaries, blackbirds, and cardinals nested in the southern part. It was a popular exhibit for fairgoers of all ages.

At the close of the fair, it was reported that the Smithsonian had plans to dismantle and move the flight cage to the zoological gardens in Washington D.C. However, St. Louis had the legal authority to buy the structure at the appraised value before other bids were considered. The city smartly acquired the unique attraction for $3,500. Although the Smithsonian lost the bird cage, it did remove most of its birds. The exhibit was replenished with acquisitions from other zoos, and some species were donated from collections of private citizens.

Flight Cage today, St. Louis Zoo

Exotic birds roost in the
giant cage.

The Flight Cage became the impetus and cornerstone for the world renowned St. Louis Zoo that grew up on adjacent parkland throughout the twentieth century. The cage marked the zoo's northeast boundary. In 1967, a major renovation project took place to repair and to restore the ever-popular attraction for future generations. The interior walkway was reintroduced and elevated for visitors to observe birds in free-flight. Further superstructure renovations were completed in 1996.

The 1904 Flight Cage looks to begin its second century with an exhibit that show-cases the native birds and animals of the Mississippi bottomlands. The focus of the Cypress Swamp exhibit is to teach visitors about the splendid and colorful birds of the Missouri and Illinois wetlands and the ecosystem in which they thrive.

The 1904 Flight Cage remains a living legacy of the great fair and continues to thrill and educate visitors of all ages.

Foursquare – Utah State Pavilion

**Utah Pavilion
1904 World's Fair**

Interior of Utah Pavilion

Utah's "stately" pavilion featured three entrances accented by double verandas that projected from the sides of this perfectly square building. This comfortable club house offered a place for relaxation. Rocking chairs and mission-style furniture invited visitors to rest, read hometown newspapers, or view hundreds of photographs of Utah's agriculture, industries, and natural resources. Members of the Mormon Church congregated at the building to recruit new members to their faith.

At the close of the fair, the tasteful furnishings in the building were sold to a country club in England at seventy-five percent of their original cost. A local stonemason purchased the building and rebuilt it on the corner of Nashville and Childress avenues in St. Louis, just south of the Forest Park fairgrounds. Although the exterior has been significantly modified, the redesign hints at the original style in the horizontal roof lines and the large front porch. The ten-room pavilion was transformed into a twelve-room residence. The original grand staircase and ten-foot French doors were incorporated into the reconstructed building, although the living space has been altered and modernized over the years.

A local neighbor recalled that early St. Louis television personality, Charlotte Peters, aired live television shows from the backyard of this once stately pavilion.

**Utah building today
St. Louis, Missouri**

Still Shining

English Domestic Style — Wisconsin State Pavilion

WORLD'S FAIR
ST. LOUIS
1904

(Postcard: Samuel Cupples Envelope Co.) Author

Photo by Yvonne Suess

**Wisconsin Pavilion, 1904 (top)
and today in Kirkwood, Missouri (bottom)**

The inviting style of the timber and stucco Wisconsin state house beckoned fair visitors to come and to relax for a while. Reminiscent of the country residences popular in both England and Germany, the building featured steep roof lines and two large pavilions at the front corners.

The two-story structure was characterized by a spacious assembly room on the first level that extended up into the second floor. Visitors had easy access to the offices and reading rooms on the ground floor while a dual staircase led to the parlors and ladies lounges on the second floor. From the rear of the pavilion, guests had a commanding view of the giant Flight Cage. The charming building with its English domestic-style architecture won a gold medal at the fair.

After the fair, the Wisconsin House was dismantled and reconstructed on Scott Avenue in Kirkwood, Missouri, just a few hundred feet from the Missouri Pacific Railroad. Although the house reflects significant redesign for residential use, it is believed that large sections of the original building were utilized. With its timber and stucco exterior, the building still hearkens back to its roots. The living room and dining room are reportedly parts of the original fair building.

In 1981, the city of Kirkwood designated the house as a historic landmark in the community.

Palace of Pines and Maples –
Buildings of the Japanese Imperial Garden

Reportedly, noted architect Frank Lloyd Wright's fascination with Japanese art and design was fueled after viewing the Japanese exhibit at the 1904 World's Fair. Shortly thereafter, he booked the first of a series of trips to Japan and that culture's artistry and architectural principles continued to influence his innovative Prairie-style designs.

The official exhibit from Japan, called the Japanese Imperial Garden, was an attractively landscaped village that featured replicas of historic buildings. Highlights included the Main Pavilion that recreated a scaled version of Kyoto's eleventh-century Imperial Palace and a pagoda based on the design of the Golden Pavilion, also of Kyoto. Other buildings at the site included the Formosa Pavilion, the Commissioners' Office, a large bazaar and several smaller shelters. All were aesthetically situated around the extensive Japanese garden, the first of its kind in the United States.

(Francis) Ronald E. Schira Collection

The Main Pavilion (right) and Bellevue Building (left)
Japanese Imperial Garden
1904 World's Fair

After the fair, the Japanese government gave three of the architectural treasures to Dr. Jokichi Takamine, a highly successful research chemist, in recognition of his work to improve relations between Japan and the United States. Dr. Takamine had the buildings dismantled, moved by rail, and reconstructed in a remote retreat in the Catskill Mountains, near Monticello,

New York. There he entertained guests at his estate in his high-roofed summer house that he named *Sho-Fu-Den*, the Palace of Pines and Maples.

Sho-Fu-Den was constructed by linking the Main Pavilion from the Japanese exhibit with the Commissioners' Office and appending one of the smaller buildings called Bellevue. Bellevue served as a reception room at the front of the house. It was built from the sixty-six species of wood native to Japan, and was originally part of the imperial family's forestry exhibit at the 1903 Osaka Exhibition. In 1904, that building was re-erected for display in St. Louis. The Commissioners' Office was remade into a bedroom and connected to the main house by an open gallery. Dr. Takamine developed the surrounding property into a twenty-acre Japanese garden.

After the doctor's death, the Moody family, who lived in the adjoining Merriewold residential colony, acquired *Sho-Fu-Den*. Later the property was sold and a restaurant operated in the building. After years of decline, Yoshitaka Ikeda purchased the property in 1986 and established the Japanese Heritage Foundation to restore the site. Foundation board members intended to convert part of the estate into a conference center, using the picturesque buildings for special gatherings.

The Secret Garden – Rhode Island State Pavilion

The Rhode Island Pavilion aptly reflected the architectural heritage of the Union's smallest state. The building was actually a composite of two elegant New England mansions, the residence built by Stephen H. Smith in the town of Lincoln, Rhode Island, and the Carrington House in Providence.

A postcard from the Rhode Island State Pavilion

The seam-faced granite exterior of the Smith mansion was convincingly recreated in cement on the Rhode Island Building. The façade was highlighted with a curved cornice of distinctive design. The booklet published by the Rhode Island Commission described the most unique feature of the building: "By ingenious arrangement of gable construction, a Roof Garden is provided, the central portion of which is shaded by the roof supported by Ionic columns, a broad stairway leading thereto from the second floor."

The pavilion's grand staircase

The Rhode Island Building was reported to be the first of the hundreds of structures at the fair to be disposed of. Although it was said to be purchased on July 4, 1904, by John Rengen for eventual transfer to his country estate, later reports cite Cyrus Blanke as the actual buyer. The building sold for $500, less than two percent of the original construction cost of $29,000. It was dismantled, loaded on horse-drawn wagons, and hauled to a site on Litzsinger Road in suburban St. Louis for rebuilding.

When reconstructed, both the interior and exterior were substantially altered. White wooden siding, since changed to gray, replaced the imitation granite covering and the roofline was redesigned with prominent dormers. The front piazza and cornice were removed, but the columns and captials were salvaged and used to decorate the corners of the house. Inside, half of the central staircase from the original building was reconstructed against a wall to save space. The modified colonial mansion is about two-thirds of the size of the building that graced the fairgrounds, but continues to recall Rhode Island's participation at the 1904 fair.

Rhode Island Building today
St. Louis County, Missouri

Modified staircase

Homestead on the Range — The Swedish Pavilion

One of the largest and best-preserved fair treasures, the Swedish Homestead Pavilion, now stands in the heart of the state of Kansas. This distinctive building located in the small town of Lindsborg recreates a typical seventeenth-century farmhouse from its Scandinavian homeland.

Swedish Pavilion, 1904 World's Fair

Ferdinand Boberg, one of Sweden's leading architects, volunteered to design the building as Sweden's hospitality center and contribution to the fair. At a cost of $17,000, the pavilion was fabricated in Sweden and reconstructed at the fair by skilled craftsmen. The building featured three unique sections in a U-shaped design. The center section housed a salon that displayed books, photographs, maps, and examples of fine Swedish furniture and vases. The east and west wings projected out beyond the center section and provided office space for Swedish dignitaries and the press. The distinctive pavilion, along with Swedish exhibit entries, won five prizes including gold, silver, and bronze medals.

At the end of the fair, the United States Minister to Sweden, W.W. Thomas Jr., purchased the pavilion. He donated the spacious building to Bethany College in the Swedish town of Lindsborg. Money was raised and the dismantled building was transported on flatbed rail cars. One old-timer remembered that the sections of the building were then loaded onto hay wagons and moved to the construction site by local farmers. From 1905 until the early 1960s, the building served students at Bethany College in a variety of ways, as a classroom, library, museum, and finally provided space for the art department. At the college, many modifications were made to the building, changing its appearance. Shingles were used to cover the exterior walls and to replace the original tile roof. The windows were modified

Staff of the Swedish Pavilion dressed in national costume

and the shutters removed. The tan pavilion turned classroom was painted red. Time and the harsh weather on the Kansas plains also took their toll on the building, which was finally determined inadequate for use by the school.

Residents of the community, however, had a sentimental attachment to the old pavilion and recognized its historical significance. The building was subsequently donated to the community's Smoky Valley Historical Association. With funding from the college, all three sections were individually moved and reunited at the McPherson County Old Mill Museum on the outskirts of Lindsborg. Restoration work was initiated to return the structure to its original appearance. In 1973, the Swedish Pavilion was placed on the National Register of Historic Places. Carl XVI Gustaf, King of Sweden, visited Lindsborg to rededicate the pavilion to all Swedes and Swedish Americans on April 17, 1976.

At the historical park, visitors can view exhibits in the spacious central hall or attend a wedding in the west wing that has been converted into a small chapel. The Swedish Pavilion continues to welcome guests as it did in 1904, but now in the middle of Kansas.

McPherson County Old Mill Museum

Restored Swedish Pavilion today
Lindsborg, Kansas

Still Shining

Buildings on the Quadrangle and Beyond — Washington University

The association between the 1904 World's Fair and the hilltop campus of Washington University in St. Louis developed out of mutual need. The fair organizers were in want of additional space for exhibits, administrative offices, and for hosting the various international congresses to be held in conjunction with the exposition. Concurrently, Washington University was seeking solutions for its funding crisis in order to complete rather than postpone construction of its new campus.

Before the turn of the twentieth century, Washington University had made plans to move the campus from its downtown location at Seventeenth Street and Washington Avenue. University administrators sought a site that was consistent with their vision to promote the school into prominence and to safeguard its location by controlling development in the surrounding area. To achieve this vision, a 108-acre tract on the western fringes of the city between Skinker and Big Bend roads was acquired, adjacent to the northwest boundary of Forest Park. In 1901, financial shortfalls threatened to halt the building program for the new campus. Funding solutions were pursued.

As plans unfolded and expanded in preparation for the fair, officials with the Louisiana Purchase Exposition Company saw the need for additional facilities. They approached Washington University in 1901 about leasing its grounds and space in its new buildings. The proposal was accepted; it saved the university from its funding crisis and met the needs of the fair. A contract was signed for $650,000. Of that sum, three additional buildings were to be erected at a total cost of $500,000 with the stipulation that they would be used first for the fair. The remaining funds were specified for grounds improvement. According to the contract, if the exposition was postponed a year to 1904, another $100,000 would be paid and an additional campus building would be constructed, also for initial use during the fair.

Photo by Nancy Schuster

Plaque commemorating Washington University's participation in the fair

Existing buildings utilized by the fair included University (Brookings) Hall, Busch Hall, Cupples Halls I and II, and the Liggett Dormitory. Lease payments from the Exposition Company funded the construction of Ridgley Building, Francis Gymnasium, Francis Field, and Tower Hall (now Umrath Hall). The Power Plant facility also served the fair from 1902 to 1905. When the exposition was delayed until 1904, the Eads physics building was quickly built with funds that were made available.

Officers of the International Congress of Arts & Sciences

(Francis) Ronald E. Schira Collection

Busch Hall, the first building completed on the campus, housed the engineers and architects of the Division of Works for the Exposition Company before being fitted as a chemistry laboratory. The Ridgley Building, named the Hall of International Congresses during the fair, was the primary location for meetings of the Congress of Arts and Sciences. That gathering of renowned scholars and scientists from around the world met in September 1904. One hundred and forty-four sessions were scheduled in the weeklong congress. Participants discussed the latest advancements in various fields of endeavor including science, philosophy, literature, art, agriculture, commerce, and labor. Many of the monographs that were presented at the conference are considered milestones in the related fields of study.

The Francis Gymnasium (known during the fair as the Physical Culture Building) and Francis Field provided athletic venues for the third Olympics of the modern era — and the first to be held on American soil.

Visiting teachers and administrators received free lodging at the Tower Hall during the summer of 1904. Washington University hoped that this hospitality would help create good publicity to generate new admissions.

With the financial boost from the fair planners, Washington University progressed through the twentieth century and into the twenty-first as an exceptional school of academic research and study. Those first campus buildings, used within the context of a world's fair to promote civic progress and to share contemporary intellectual thought, have continued to provide students with leading-edge educational opportunities to benefit the community and the world.

During the fair, University Hall (above) served as the Administration Building for the Louisiana Purchase Exposition Company.

Named after its benefactor, Robert S. Brookings Hall (right) today houses the administrative offices for Washington University.

The Board of Lady Managers (bottom left) for the Louisiana Purchase Exposition, authorized by Congress, had the foremost duty to award prizes to women who submitted entries for competitive exhibits. Eads Hall (top) served as the board's official headquarters. The building was constructed in 1902 and was a gift to Washington University from Mrs. James Finney How. She was the daughter of engineer and bridge builder, James Eads, for whom the building is named. Eads Hall (bottom right) later housed the university's physics department.

Cupples I (above) was named after Samuel Cupples, the official stationer of the fair and donor of the building. On the north side of the quadrangle, it served as the Anthropology Building for the exposition.

The first building on the hilltop campus continues to bear the name of its benefactor, Adolphus Busch. The engineers and architects of the fair's Division of Works used Busch Hall (left) as their headquarters.

Still Shining

Originally known as Liggett Hall (left), the building was built in 1901 with the financial support of Mrs. Elizabeth J. Liggett and named in honor of her late husband, John E. Liggett. It served as the first men's dormitory to house fair personnel. Today, the building is known as Prince Hall.

Tower Hall (right) was constructed using the money that the Exposition Company paid to lease the campus buildings for the fair. Built in 1902, it served as the second men's dormitory. The hall was renamed Lee Hall in 1929 and changed to Umrath Hall in 1963.

Cupples II (left) was constructed in 1901 as the first building off the quadrangle. It was also a gift of Samuel Cupples and used for the engineering school. During the fair, the Jefferson Guard (below) established its headquarters there. A second engineering building, the Cupples Engineering Laboratory, was connected to Cupples II and provided warehouse space for the exposition. The building was razed in 1967.

Built in 1901, the Ridgley Building (right) faces University (Brookings) Hall on the quadrangle. During the fair, the building was known as the International Hall of Congresses and the learned minds of the world met within its confines. Delegates assembled here during the 1904 Democratic Convention. Queen Victoria's Jubilee gifts were displayed on the first floor. Rental income from the exposition financed the completion of the Ridgley Building, later used as a library.

The Physical Culture Building and the adjacent athletic field (later named Francis Field for the president of the exposition, David R. Francis) served as the venues for the third Olympic Games. The building contained gymnastic facilities. The track and field events were contested on the athletic field as spectators watched from the stadium bleachers. Rental payments from the exposition paid for both the building and field with its concrete bleachers. The Aeronautics Competition was held nearby on the university grounds. Contestants were challenged to follow a prescribed course at a speed of at least twenty miles per hour to qualify for prizes.

Physical Culture Building at the 1904 Olympic Games

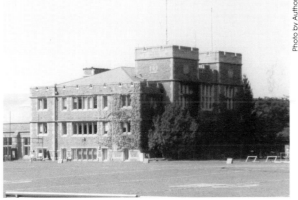

Francis Gymnasium today

1904 Olympic marathoners in front of stadium bleachers

Francis Field track and bleachers today

Sculpture & Statuary

The fancy of the sculptor has been given the wildest latitude, and allegory reaches the boldest flights of imagination. Beginning with the decoration of Festival Hall, the sculptural masses portray the liveliest and most extravagant symbols of pleasure and pure abandon.

Official Guide to the Louisiana Purchase Exposition

The Stroke of the Pen — *Signing of the Treaty*

The tall shaft of the Louisiana Purchase Monument stood at the northeast end of the Grand Basin in tribute to Thomas Jefferson's acquisition of the Louisiana Territory, the great sweep of land that more than doubled the size of the country in 1803. The three diplomats who executed the Louisiana Purchase Treaty were depicted at the base of the monument in a high relief sculpture, designed and created in staff by Karl Bitter, the chief sculptor of the exhibition.

Bitter's representation showed the final moment in the effort to acquire the Louisiana Territory — the signing of the treaty by French Minister François Marquis De Barbe-Marbois. American Ambassador Robert Livingston and his assistant, future president James Monroe, look on observing the success of their efforts.

The treaty was the culmination of negotiations between Jefferson's administration and Napoleon's government. Although still under Spanish control, Spain had secretly ceded Louisiana and New Orleans to France in 1800. Jefferson knew that the Port of New Orleans needed to be secured to control commerce on the Mississippi River.

With France on the verge of war with England, Napoleon surprisingly offered the huge tract of land for purchase. France sold not only the port, but the entire Louisiana Territory to the United States, to

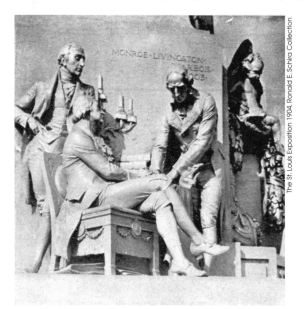

Signing of the Treaty represented the acquisition of the Louisiana Territory.

The sculpture rested at the base of the Louisiana Purchase Monument.

fund its war effort and to avoid the risk of losing the territory in the conflict. Although the United States Constitution made no provision for land acquisition to expand the nation, Jefferson took the bold step to authorize the purchase. The treaty was signed on April 30, 1903, opening the gates for westward expansion. Exactly 101 years later, St. Louis opened the gates to the Louisiana Purchase Exposition on April 30, 1904, to commemorate that historic event that changed the face of the nation.

Two bronze casts of the Bitter sculpture were authorized after the fair. One stands appropriately in the state capital of Missouri, Jefferson City, named in honor of our third president. The sculpture is the focal point of a stone monument erected on an overlook of the Missouri River, the mighty waterway that passes through several of the states carved from the Louisiana Territory. The other cast was unveiled in 1913 in the loggia at the Jefferson Memorial in St. Louis' Forest Park, the current home of the Missouri History Museum.

In 1953, the sculpture group was portrayed on a stamp issued by the U. S. Post Office to commemorate the sesquicentennial of the Louisiana Purchase.

Signing of the Treaty
Missouri River Overlook
Jefferson City, Missouri

Bronze cast of Signing of the Treaty
Missouri History Museum
St. Louis, Missouri

Just to Think — Rodin's *The Thinker*

Posed in contemplation for the ages, *The Thinker*, a signature work of Auguste Rodin (1840-1917), must have intrigued fair visitors and elicited a multitude of interpretations. The larger-than-life-size statue, however, began on a much smaller scale.

Gates of Hell by Auguste Rodin

Inscription: "*The Thinker* by Auguste Rodin — A Gift to the People of Louisville by the Hillman-Hopkins Family MCMXLIX"

Working in a factory as a china painter, it was not until 1880 that Rodin was commissioned by the French government to design bronze doors of massive size for a decorative-arts museum. Rodin chose to depict Dante's *Divine Comedy* in the complex design known as the *Gates of Hell*. Directly above the two doors, he modeled Dante, the poet, as *The Thinker*.

When the museum project failed, Rodin chose to enlarge some of the figures on the gates for future sales and exhibits. Rodin worked with Henri Lebosse, a professional reproducer, to mechanically enlarge the figure of Dante from the twenty-seven-inch model to a six-foot, seven-inch sitting figure. The first enlargement was cast in bronze by A. A. Hebrard in the complicated and costly lost-wax method. Despite defects noted by Rodin, Hebrard was eager to show his successful cast, and it was sent to St. Louis for display at the 1904 World's Fair. Fairgoers could view this colossal figure, which has become one of the world's most famous and recognized sculptures.

The Thinker displayed at the 1904 fair was the first of twenty-one period casts authorized by Rodin. After the fair, the statue was acquired by Henry Walters, founder of the Walters Art Gallery of Baltimore. Walters displayed Rodin's masterpiece in the courtyard of his home that he built to house his art collection. In 1949, eighteen years after Walters' death, the gallery sold The Thinker to the estate of Louisville attorney, Arthur E. Hopkins. Hopkins had stipulated the purchase of three bronze statues in his will including a cast of The Thinker. Although the will specified the purchase of the Rodin sculpture from the French government, executors of the Hopkins estate elected to purchase the work from the Walters Gallery as being in the best interest of the city of Louisville, the recipient of the sculpture. Trustees at the Walters Gallery agreed to sell the statue because the Baltimore Museum of Art had a cast also. The site chosen to display the gift was in front of the Administration Building at the University of Louisville, where it stands (or sits) in thought today.

The Metropolitan Museum of Art in New York City owns a plaster cast of The Thinker that was also displayed at the 1904 fair.

Revolutionary Disciplinarian —
Baron Friedrich Wilhelm von Steuben

Baron Friedrich Wilhelm von Steuben Palace of Varied Industries 1904 World's Fair

Shaded by a grove of gingko trees behind the Victorian pond in St. Louis' Tower Grove Park is a bronze sculpture of Baron Friedrich Wilhelm von Steuben. The statue of this Prussian nobleman and military leader is in tribute to his service as George Washington's drillmaster and aide de camp during the Revolutionary War. Sent by Emperor Frederick the Great, von Steuben laid the foundations for training and discipline of the citizen soldiers who fought for American independence.

The statue was originally commissioned by Kaiser Wilhelm II's imperial government and later displayed at the fair. Standing approximately five feet tall, it was a model for a proposed monument and was cast at a foundry in Lauchhammer, Germany. That foundry created many statues of Germans and German-Americans during the late nineteenth and early twentieth centuries for installation in cities that celebrated their German heritage. The von Steuben statue was displayed in the Palace of Varied Industries as an example of fine German foundry work for commissions rather than as a competitive entry. It depicts the confident leader in military dress with a young recruit at his feet.

The statue today Tower Grove Park St. Louis, Missouri

When the fair closed, August A. Busch Sr. purchased the statue for one hundred dollars. It was retrieved from storage after World War I and moved to a place of prominence in front of the Bevo Mill restaurant in South St. Louis. The statue was subsequently sold to a retired undertaker who used it as lawn ornamentation. His widow appropriately donated the bronze to the St. Louis von Steuben Society, which displayed it on a marble base at the old Liederkrantz Hall on South Grand Boulevard. In 1968, the Society offered the statue to Tower Grove Park for installation on a new granite base that it also provided.

Still Shining

At the Gates — *Fountain Angel*

Visitors entering the fair at the Lindell-Skinker gate were greeted by the graceful *Fountain Angel* created by Florentine sculptor Raffaello Romanelli. With outstretched arms, the bronze angel delicately held two ewers and water gently flowed from each. The base of the statue was accented by four large dog heads; their open mouths served as water spouts. The figure may have represented Persephone, a Greek goddess of the underworld. The sculpture was part of a larger fountain setting at the fair. A marble column rose behind the statue with water flowing from an overhead basin.

Lindell-Kingshighway entrance to Forest Park (after the fair)

***Fountain Angel*
Missouri Botanical Garden**

At the close of the fair, the sculpture would continue to welcome visitors to Forest Park. David N. O'Neil purchased the fountain and presented it as a gift to the City of St. Louis in memory of his father, Judge Joseph O'Neil, who served on the board of Forest Park commissioners in 1874. The sculpture was installed at the park's Lindell-Kingshighway entrance in 1907, but was relocated to the interior of the park in 1916, just south of the Field House. The Parks Department placed the statue in storage for years after it was vandalized in the 1960s.

In 1975, the statue was restored and installed at the Missouri Botanical Garden in St. Louis. Today it can be seen just west of Henry Shaw's Tower Grove House in a circular pool that graces the Victorian gardens surrounding the home.

Birmingham's Giant on the Hill – *Vulcan*

Massive sculpture of a historical or allegorical theme was not only displayed for its artistic merit, but also to promote industry and agriculture. In this regard, the Commercial Club of the city of Birmingham, Alabama, responded to an invitation from the fair organizers with a monolithic cast-iron statue. It depicted Vulcan, the mythological god of fire and forge. Fabricated of native iron, it was an advertisement promoting Birmingham's major industry, iron and steel manufacturing.

(Benriff) Author

**Vulcan
1904 World's Fair**

The contract to fabricate Vulcan was signed November 21, 1903, just five months before the fair was to open. To raise funds for the project, twelve-inch-tall statuettes of Vulcan were produced in bronze. Sales were brisk in Birmingham and later at the fair. The *Birmingham Age-Herald* reported in its June 2, 1904, edition, "Many ladies are purchasing two of them and placing them at either end of the mantels in their homes."

Photo by Author

To complete the world's largest cast-iron statue within the tight time frame, the sculptor, Giuseppe Moretti, needed a building large enough to create the plaster model. An unfinished church in Passaic, New Jersey, served the purpose. In March 1904, iron molders at the Birmingham Steel and Iron Company began the fabrication of the statue from sections of the plaster form shipped from New Jersey. By mid-April, seven railway cars were loaded with the large sections of Vulcan for assembly at the fair. The parts were welded together and construction was completed by late May.

At a height of fifty-six feet, Vulcan stood with commanding presence in the Palace of Mines and Metallurgy. His triumphant pose saluted the discovery of iron. Moretti correctly portrayed Vulcan as a laboring blacksmith with a rugged, almost ugly countenance holding a spear just forged from his anvil. An international panel of judges awarded the

**Vulcan
Birmingham, Alabama**

Vulcan statuette

"Iron Man" a grand prize and presented medals to Moretti and to James R. McWane, who did the casting. At the conclusion of the fair, the statue was taken apart and transported back to Birmingham. Controversy surrounded plans to re-erect it in a downtown park bordered by an elite residential neighborhood. While Vulcan was admired at the fair, many residents thought the partially clothed colossus belonged elsewhere. It would be years before Vulcan would find a home near his origins — on Red Mountain, Birmingham's iron ore reserve.

In 1906, Vulcan was removed from storage and reconstructed at the Alabama State Fairgrounds. The giant's left hand was incorrectly positioned and unable to hold his hammer. Vendors on the fairgrounds seized the opportunity to use Vulcan to advertise their products by placing fabricated ice cream cones or soft drinks in his empty hand. Vulcan also hawked pickles and once sported overalls as a promotional gimmick

In 1939, Vulcan's dignity was restored. He was given a permanent home atop Red Mountain in a park overlooking the city of Birmingham. Plans for that relocation began in 1935 and were accomplished as a WPA project during the next few years. Vulcan was placed on a 120-foot octagonal tower with an open-air observation platform accessible by a 160-step staircase.

Vulcan's role changed in 1946 from a sentinel to a beacon over the city. His uplifted spear was replaced by a torch to serve as a traffic safety reminder. It burned red on any day with a traffic fatality and green on days without one. From 1969-1971, the Vulcan site was modernized. The tall tower was covered with white-polished marble and an external elevator was added. The observation platform was enlarged and enclosed, still affording a breathtaking view of the city, but eliminating a close-up view of the man of iron.

Over the years, weather, age, and the structural modifications to install the giant on the hill have taken their toll. Restoration efforts have been again initiated for the statue and the surrounding park, so that Vulcan may long stand as a symbol of Birmingham's industrial roots.

Vulcan during restoration
Birmingham, Alabama

Copies of the Classics —
Gerber-Houck Statuary Collection

One of the hallmarks of the Louisiana Purchase Exposition was the abundance of statuary displayed throughout the fairgrounds. The German Educational Exhibit was no exception. A valuable collection of elegant statuary — replicas of ancient, medieval, and modern works of art by a noted Cologne artist, August Gerber — was awarded a Grand Prize at the fair. Gerber's reproductions, made of a secret plaster substance that included alabaster, were hand-rubbed with bees-wax and buffed to give the statues the illusion of a marble, stone, or bronze finish. Each statue was the same size as its original museum piece displayed in Europe. Free-standing statues, relief sculptures, and busts comprised the display. The entire collection of fifty-eight pieces could be viewed in the German Sections of the Palace of Liberal Arts and at the Education and Social Economy Building.

Inspired by the elegant statuary, Louis Houck of Cape Girardeau, Missouri, was determined to bring these replicas of some of the world's most important artwork to the Southeast Missouri Normal School. Houck, a member of the school's Board of Regents, purchased the collection for $1,500 and presented it as a gift. The statuary was transported to Cape Girardeau by river barge, and horse and wagon.

German Educational Exhibit. St. Louis Art Museum Library/Archives

Gerber's statuary replicas at the entrance to the German section in the Palace of Liberal Arts

Gerber personally installed the artwork at the school in 1905. For many years, the statuary could be viewed in Statuary Hall just as Gerber had arranged it. By the mid-1950s, the growing student population demanded part of the space for classrooms and offices of the now Southeast Missouri State College. In 1958, the collection was dispersed and the sculptures were placed near those academic departments to which their study was relevant. As the statues were scattered, the lack of consistent care and supervision took its toll. Some pieces were misplaced, vandalized, or even broken beyond repair. Interest in the statuary faded.

Photo by Yvonne Suess

In 1976 and 1977, the fate of the statuary was reversed. The historic significance of the replicas spurred a comprehensive effort to reassemble, research, and repair the collection. Pieces were resurrected from the library basement, an elevator shaft, and the backstage area of the college's auditorium. The restoration process involved research in art history books so that repairs could be made accurately. Hands and fingers needed to be fashioned, and chips and cracks tediously filled. Each statue was sanded and painted to resemble the original alabaster finish. Two of the busts (titled *Bambinos*) did not require repainting and still reflect the original patina.

Forty-two sculptures were reclaimed from the original collection. These refurbished pieces are displayed at the campus museum at Southeast Missouri State University. Part of the original carved brass railing that safeguarded the exhibit at the fair in 1904 again accents the display and protects it today.

Restored Gerber-Houck statuary replicas
Southeast Missouri State University
Cape Girardeau, Missouri

Looking Homeward — *Forest Devotion*

Beer manufacturing giant August A. Busch Sr. chose his final resting place at Sunset Memorial Park in St. Louis County on a hilltop that affords a view of his family's Grant's Farm estate.

The Greatest of Expositions, Author

Forest Devotion
German Country House, 1904

Photo by Author

Forest Devotion
Busch gravesite, St. Louis County

A rough granite boulder bearing the Busch name marks the family gravesite and is the base for a graceful bronze statue that completes the monument. Known as *Forest Devotion*, the statue suggests man's union with nature by depicting a boy gently offering a fawn a drink from a small dish. Josef Hinterseher created the work.

The statue was originally displayed within the open court of the German Country House at the fair's Palace of Varied Industries. Garden courts, accented by water pools, plantings, and statuary, were typical of the style that wealthy Germans were incorporating into their country homes at the turn of the twentieth century.

Center Court — Meet Me at *The Eagle*

Germany paid tribute to the national symbol of the United States by installing an American eagle of massive size as the centerpiece in its Court of Honor at the Palace of Varied Industries. Handcrafted for the fair, each of the five thousand bronze feathers was individually molded, hammered, and fitted into place by master craftsmen. The huge raptor stood over six feet tall. Perched atop a pedestal of equal size, it was the focal point of the exhibit hall.

The Eagle, designed by August Gaul of Berlin
Palace of Varied Industries, 1904 World's Fair

The Eagle, Lord & Talyor Department Store
Philadelphia, Pennsylvania

At the close of the exposition, John Wanamaker acquired this spectacular specimen of modern metal art for his flagship department store that bore his name for decades in downtown Philadelphia. At 2,500 pounds, the floor beneath the statue required steel bracing before installation. The eagle became the symbol for Wanamaker's cutting-edge retail business. The stately bird continues to dominate the Grand Count of the store, now under the Lord & Taylor name. As a popular gathering spot, "Meet me at the Eagle" has been the call of Philadelphia shoppers for years.

Southern Honors — *General Albert Sidney Johnston Memorial*

The state of Texas and sculptor Elisabet Ney chose to honor one of the state's patriots, General Albert Sidney Johnston, within the art exhibits at the St. Louis World's Fair.

General Johnston was held in highest regard because of his service to Texas and his distinguished military career. During the Civil War, Confederacy President Jefferson Davis recognized the qualities of this fine soldier and stated, "I hoped and expected that I had others who would prove generals, but I knew I had one, and that was Sidney Johnston."

Max Storm Collection

**Texas State building
1904 World's Fair**

A West Point graduate in 1826, Johnston resigned his commission after eight years to care for his seriously ill wife. Shortly after her death, he was inspired by a speech given by Stephen Austin advocating the fight for Texas independence from Mexico. Joining the Texas revolutionary army as a private, his talents were quickly revealed. Within a year, he rose to the rank of senior brigadier and was placed in command of the army. After Texas independence, Johnston served as the Secretary of War for the new republic. He continued to fight for Texas during the Mexican War as the Commander of the First Texas Rifle Volunteers and later served in the U. S. Army during the antebellum period with assignments on the western frontier. In 1857, he was promoted to brigadier general by brevet.

General Johnston joined the Confederate Army in August 1861 and assumed command of the western theater of operations. Abandoning the defensive lines in Kentucky and most of Tennessee, Johnston met his fate at the Battle of Shiloh in 1862. While leading a final charge against Union forces, he was wounded by a bullet that severed an artery in his leg. Lacking medical attention, he bled to death from the battle wound having ordered his surgeon to attend to injured federal prisoners.

The Texas Division of the United Daughters of the Confederacy chose to commemorate the heroic deeds of General Johnston by creating an appropriate memorial to him. They selected Elisabet Ney, a talented artist with a rebellious flair who became a Texas transplant after leaving Germany — and the court of half-mad King Ludwig. In 1900, Ney completed a plaster model of the general in repose. Her portrayal depicted the general in his Confederate Army uniform lying on a stretcher after the battle of Shiloh. His head rests on the Lone Star flag, and his body is draped with the flag of the Confederacy.

In 1902, with funding in place, the commission was awarded and the marble statue of the general was carved by Italian stonecutters. The sculpture was finished in the spring of 1904, just in time to be shipped to St. Louis for display in the Palace of Art at the fair. Among the works that Ney had selected for display at the exposition in both the Palace of Art and in the Texas State Building, she was most proud of her sculpture of General Johnston.

Judges recognized Elisabet Ney's artistry with a bronze medal. The sculpture was fittingly returned to Texas after the fair and installed to mark the general's grave at the Texas State Cemetery in Austin. The monument to this esteemed soldier is protected today by a steel rail and plexiglass enclosure under a gothic canopy, also designed by the sculptor.

The plaster cast of this sculpture, reportedly displayed within the fair's Texas Building, is now in the collection of the Elisabet Ney Museum in Austin, Texas.

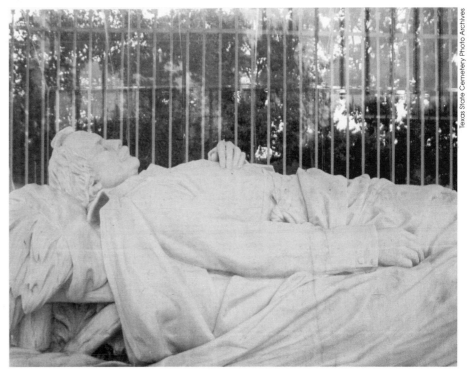

Texas State Cemetery Photo Archives

***General Albert Sidney Johnston Memorial* today**
Texas State Cemetery, Austin, Texas

Water Nymphs – *The Wrestling Bacchantes*

When charismatic entrepreneur and developer Edward Gardner Lewis founded the St. Louis suburb of University City in 1902, he envisioned a planned community that would be the headquarters for his publishing business, but more importantly, a national center for art and education. For the next decade, he executed his plan to build a model city by erecting a publishing plant for his *Woman's Magazine*, designing an elegant subdivision, and founding the American Woman's League (a rural woman's organization) and its affiliated People's University. Among the course offerings at the school, there was an emphasis on the arts — and Lewis attracted gifted artists, sculptors, and ceramicists as instructors for his Academy of Fine Arts.

**Wrestling Bacchantes
(second from left)
Academy of Fine Arts, Statuary Hall**

**Wrestling Bacchantes
1904 World's Fair**

Lewis won the admiration of many for his commitment to artistic expression and many valuable statues were presented to the League's Art Academy. This included the Cararra marble statue titled *Wrestling Bacchantes* by the Italian sculptor Petrilla. Reportedly displayed at the 1904 World's Fair by the Italian Government, it was purchased by Mr. L. J. W. Wall for placement in Statuary Hall at the League's Art Academy.

After accusations of business improprieties and the demise of his art and education center, Lewis departed in 1912 to pursue his dream in California. He founded the Atascadero Colony (now the city of Atascadero, California) in 1913 with visions of incorporating the "utopian ideals" that failed in his University City effort. As investors came to settle in the new community, Lewis first housed them in a "tent city," an idea that he also used in University City to provide low-cost lodging for visitors to the nearby fair in 1904. Permanent structures were erected as the Atascadero community developed. The Colony Administration Building was constructed between 1914 and 1918. The sculpture of the *Wrestling Bacchantes* was transported across the country and was installed as public art near the fledgling community's new commercial and social center known as La Plaza, not far from the Administration Building. The installation of the statue is recounted in *The Birth of Atascadero* by Marguerite A. Travis:

> It was also in 1916 … that the beautiful Carrarra (sic) marble group, "The Three Bathing Girls," was unveiled and mounted in the parkway across the highway from the Administration Building. This piece of statuary, one of the nation's art treasures, made from one solid block of white Carrara (sic) marble, had been the chief exhibit of the Italian government at the St. Louis World's Fair in 1903 (sic). It weighed 2400 pounds and was awarded grand prize at the Exposition.
>
> The Italian government paid $27,000 to the sculptor who created it, and the group was considered one of the finest works of art in this country when it was exhibited in St. Louis.

Although the sculpture attracted considerable attention during the World's Fair, not all found the work completely acceptable. When Lewis' Academy of Fine Arts in University City was sold, Taxile Doat, the former pottery artist at the Academy, wrote in a letter dated March 17, 1915, to William Victor Bragdon, "the art building is sold and next the High School will occupy it, but myself I hope they will take out the marble group — Bacchants (sic). That subject is not for young girls. Bachelors will have some pleasure to contemplate it but is not a subject for High School."

The Administration Building of the Atascadero Colony remains today. It is a registered California Historical Landmark that serves the community as City Hall, local museum, and site of the *Wrestling Bacchantes*, now popularly nicknamed *The Water Nymphs*.

Photo by Susan Beatie

Wrestling Bacchantes nicknamed *Water Nymphs*
Atascadero, California

Galloping for Gold – *The Mares of Diomedes*

H is most notable achievement was the colossal carving from 1927 to 1941 of Washington, Lincoln, Jefferson, and Theodore Roosevelt on Mount Rushmore. But at the 1904 St. Louis World's Fair, Gutzon Borglum won a gold medal for one of his earlier works. A wild equine group with the energy of a stampede, his bronze sculpture bore the classical title, *The Horses of Diomedes* (now titled *The Mares of Diomedes)*, from the mythological legend, *The Labors of Hercules.*

Borglum's early sculptures were influenced by his upbringing in the American West and the works of world-renowned sculptor, Auguste Rodin, whom he met while studying art and working in Paris. The exposition's publication titled *The Art Department Illustrated* describes the sculpture as "one of Mr. Borglum's first large and complex pieces. … In conception it is most original, exceedingly well composed, and the execution shows not only great ability in handling, but also an extensive knowledge of the horse."

Today, *The Mares of Diomedes* is in the collection of the Metropolitan Museum of Art in New York City and is noteworthy as the museum's first purchase of an American sculpture.

The Mares of Diomedes
1904 World's Fair

The Mares of Diomedes (foreground, right)
Palace of Art, Grand Court
1904 World's Fair

Silent Music — *The Florentine Singer*

The youthful *Florentine Singer*, displayed at the 1904 fair, now finds peaceful repose at the Valhalla Mausoleum on St. Charles Rock Road in suburban St. Louis. It stands on a low pedestal above a fountain and pool.

This bronze figure of a young man playing a mandolin is an original piece by French sculptor, Paul Du Bois. Works by Du Bois are noteworthy. They are displayed in some of the world's largest museums, including the Musée d'Orsay, which has a silvered-bronze version of the *Florentine Singer*.

Valhalla's Art Committee acquired the sculpture in 1939.

The Florentine Singer
St. Louis County, Missouri

Treasures from the Orient – Japanese Eagle and Vase

Two artistic gems from the Japanese exhibits at the fair continue to give a glimpse of the artistry of that Far Eastern culture.

The Japanese Embassy brought a superb sculpture piece from the Orient — a magnificent bronze eagle that once stood guard in the courtyard of a Japanese temple. Created during the eighteenth century, the eagle with its fourteen-foot wing-span is a study in realism.

The J.C. Nichols Company acquired the sculpture from a New York art dealer in 1935 and donated it to the people of Kansas City, Missouri. Restored with contributions from patrons at $350 for a feather or $50 for a pinion, the two-ton eagle alights on Ward Parkway at 67th Street in south Kansas City.

**Japanese Eagle
Kansas City, Missouri**

**A close-up of the Japanese Eagle
Kansas City, Missouri**

A large Japanese vase, acquired from the fair, decorates the lobby of the Ziegenhein Funeral Home on Gravois Road in historic South St. Louis. The enameled vase stands forty inches tall and combines Japanese figures within the floral design.

Photo by Yvonne Suess

(Bennitt/1904 LPE CD) Philip Geerling

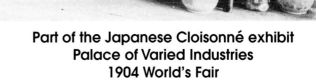

Japanese Vase with detail
St. Louis, Missouri

Photo by Yvonne Suess

Part of the Japanese Cloisonné exhibit
Palace of Varied Industries
1904 World's Fair

Exhibit Items ... and More

"The finished array of exhibits as set forth in the various exhibit palaces and elsewhere constituted a complete record in actual reproduction of the capacity and performance of the modern world. It was a comprehensive collection of the best works of man and the best collective products of society — a full and accurate reflection of civilization in its perfection as reached at the beginning of the twentieth century. ... The scope and diversity of the exhibits offered in each building were stupendous."

David R. Francis
The Universal Exposition of 1904

Expansion and Education — Thomas Jefferson's Headstone

A rough-hewn granite obelisk in the Palace of Education was the gathering point for dignitaries who assembled to celebrate Virginia Day at the fair on September 22. The monument once stood to mark the gravesite of Thomas Jefferson, but was not obtained for the exposition from his Monticello estate, but from the University of Missouri–Columbia. The history behind the grave marker and its eventual relocation to Missouri is intriguing.

In his personal papers, Jefferson left instructions for the design of his tombstone. Penned on the back of an envelope, he provided the specifications and a sketch for the simple monument that he desired.

Thomas Jefferson's headstone at the University of Missouri–Columbia

"On the grave, a plain die or cube of 3 feet, without any mouldings, surmounted by an obelisk of 6 feet height, each of a single stone. On the faces of obelisk the following inscription, and not a word more:

> *'Here was buried*
> *Thomas Jefferson*
> *Author of the Declaration of American Independence*
> *of the Statute of Virginia for religious freedom*
> *& Father of the University of Virginia.'*

because by these, as testimonials that I have lived, I wish most to be remembered. To be of the coarse stone of which my columns are made, that no one might be tempted hereafter to destroy it for the value of the materials. . . . On the die of the obelisk might be engraved:

> *'BORN APRIL 2, 1743, O.S.*
> *DIED ?'"*

Jefferson's descendants followed his wishes and had the stone monument cut and installed over his grave at Monticello. The inscription, however, was carved into a marble plaque that was attached to the marker.

Jefferson's heirs subsequently sold his estate to pay off the significant debts that had accrued. The graveyard fell into disrepair and into the hands of vandals and souvenir seekers who chipped splinters from the granite tombstone. In 1882, after several earlier efforts to address the situation, Congress appropriated $10,000 to renovate the graveyard and to erect a new monument to the great president who had served his country in so many capacities. The new eight-ton monument was dedicated in 1883.

Jefferson's descendants reviewed many requests for relocating the original headstone. The University of Missouri–Columbia submitted a request with a threefold justification. It stated that the purchase of the Louisiana Territory was one of Jefferson's greatest accomplishments, that the state of Missouri was carved from the territory, and that the university was the first state university founded in the territory — with even a philosophy similar to that of Jefferson's University of Virginia. After careful consideration of the requests, the descendants determined the University of Missouri as the most fitting site to relocate the headstone and to honor the former president. In an elaborate ceremony, the Jefferson monument was unveiled on July 4, 1885, in front of Academic Hall, the main campus building. University administrators subsequently removed the inscribed marble plaque and placed it inside Academic Hall to safeguard it. Ironically, fire destroyed the building in 1892, but the Jefferson monument escaped harm. The marble plaque, however, was fractured and charred, but has since been restored.

Over the years, Jefferson's monument has been relocated several times on the campus. In 1904, the historic tombstone was displayed in the Palace of Education at the St. Louis Fair, in memory of the president who acquired the Louisiana Territory and had a keen interest in the education of the citizenry — the underlying themes of the fair.

In his *Universal Exposition of 1904*, David R. Francis recalls the gathering on Virginia Day at the fair:

> *Jefferson may easily be regarded as the patron spirit of the Exposition. The reverential visitors from the Old Dominion gathered around the granite monument which so long marked the grave at Monticello, and like the knights of old, refreshed their memories and renewed their loyal admiration at this plain and rugged shrine. Fitting it was that the gravestone of Thomas Jefferson, Father of the University of Virginia, should stand during the Exposition among the exhibits in the palace of Education.*

The planners of the Jamestown Exposition (1907) may have thought a precedent had been set and requested the monument for display at that upcoming fair. The curators at the university, however, declined the request for fear that the hallowed obelisk may never be returned from Virginia.

The tombstone was rededicated in 1932 with the addition of a replacement panel inscribed with Jefferson's epitaph. In 1976, during America's bicentennial celebration, the monument was moved again to a more prominent location on the campus. It stands there today next to the chancellor's residence along a walkway in the Francis Quadrangle.

Jefferson's monument at the University of Missouri symbolizes his vision of westward expansion and his belief in education for all people.

Students pass by Jefferson's headstone at the University of Missouri–Columbia.

From Palace to Pub — Chandeliers at O'Connell's

German Educational Exhibit, St. Louis Art Museum Library and Archives

**Banquet Hall
British Pavilion
1904 World's Fair**

Great Britain's entry at the 1904 fair was a faithful reproduction of the Orangery, the banqueting hall at Kensington Palace in London, designed for Queen Anne by world-renowned architect Christopher Wren. According to legend, the Orangery gained its name after the queen first viewed oranges growing in its courtyard. At the fair, two wings adjoined the main banquet hall and housed an Elizabethan breakfast room, a Georgian dining room, the Adams tea room, a reception room, and offices. The Orangery was located on Skinker Road just to the left of the main drive leading to the exposition's Administration Building (now Robert S. Brookings Hall). Built to resemble red brick, the building was not razed at the conclusion of the fair. Rather, it was purchased by Washington University and served as "temporary quarters" for the art school. It was used from 1909 until 1926 when Bixby Hall was completed. Bixby Hall was even designed to incorporate some of the finely crafted materials from the interior of the British Pavilion, especially the wood paneling.

Reportedly, the candelabra chandeliers from the banquet hall were placed into storage before the building was demolished. Later, they were sold to an antique dealer and subsequently reappeared in two fabled establishments of St. Louis' bygone entertainment district known as Gaslight Square. O'Connell's Pub and the Three Fountains restaurant lit their businesses with these multi-tiered, eighteen-light fixtures. Each establishment had two of the large brass chandeliers.

The fate of the lights after the closure of the Three Fountains restaurant is unknown. When O'Connell's Pub moved to Shaw Avenue at Kingshighway Boulevard in St. Louis, however, the elegant chandeliers were reinstalled at the new location. Patrons in the bar now sit in the soft glow of these banquet hall lights, so large that the long support shafts needed to be pulled up through the pressed metal ceiling.

Photo by Author

**British Pavilion
chandeliers at
O'Connell's Pub
St. Louis, Missouri**

Photo by Author

Lighting the Way — Snow-viewing Lanterns from the Japanese Imperial Garden

St. Louis is currently home to one of the largest Japanese-style gardens outside of the country of Japan. But in 1904, the Japanese introduced fair visitors to the beauty of oriental landscaping by inviting them to stroll though its Imperial Garden and traditional buildings. Today, St. Louis' world-renowned Missouri Botanical Garden invites tourists from across the globe to visit *Seiwa-en*, "Garden of pure, clear harmony and peace." Two treasures from the first Japanese garden in North America, featured at the St. Louis World's Fair, sowed the seeds for the future development of *Seiwa-en*.

At the fair, several acres were aesthetically landscaped to create a garden in typical Japanese design. Winding pathways led visitors through foliage and flowering plants. Picturesque bridges and stepping stone pavers provided crossings over little streams while fountains splashed and waterfalls tumbled nearby.

(Bennitt) Author

**Japanese Imperial Garden
1904 World's Fair**

Carved stone lanterns, that have lit Japanese temples and gardens for centuries, accented the imperial landscape recreated in St. Louis in 1904. Two of these Japanese lanterns from the fairground continue their traditional function today and can be seen at *Seiwa-en* at the Missouri Botanical Garden. They were purchased by Leonard Matthews after the fair and were used to decorate his own garden on Cabanne Avenue in St. Louis. Sometime before 1930, they were donated to the Missouri Botanical Garden.

The lanterns actually prompted dreams of a Japanese garden after they were acquired by the Missouri Botanical Garden, a dream that became reality when *Seiwa-en* was dedicated in 1977.

Both lanterns are *yukimi doro* or snow-viewing lanterns. Today, one is found within the dry garden at the entrance to *Seiwa-en*, while the other is nestled under a grove of trees along a side pathway. The graceful lanterns are designed to blend subtly with the tranquil landscape. Each contains a hexagonal compartment to hold a lamp or candle covered by a broad cap. The caps are designed to display snow, which the Japanese believe to be a flower of winter, called *sekka* or *toka*. Many of the plantings and garden ornaments in the Japanese Garden are to be appreciated in all seasons, even in winter by the way the snow accumulates and outlines their gentle contours.

Photo by Author

Japanese Garden, *Seiwa-en*
St. Louis, Missouri

Photo by Author

Photo by Author

Photo by Barbara Uhl

1904 Japanese Lanterns
Missouri Botanical Garden
St. Louis, Missouri

The One and — "Owney"

"OWNEY," THE RAILWAY MAIL DOG.

For years "Owney" was a pet of the Railway Mail Service, traveling thousands of miles in postal cars and accumulating tags and medals of all kinds. After his death he was stuffed and exhibited by the Post Office Department at the Exposition.

Owney at the 1904 World's Fair

(Bennitt) Max Storm Collection

Perhaps the most famous dog of the late nineteenth century was Owney, mascot of the Railway Mail Service. His was a lifetime of adventure and travel, as he hitched rides on the mail trains that crisscrossed the country.

Owney's career with the United States Post Office Department began in 1888 when he wandered into the Albany Post Office in New York and nestled on a bed of mail bags. Mail clerks soon adopted the friendly terrier and gave him a home. Owney never strayed far from mailbags after that. He traveled freely to cities and towns across the country, guarding mail pouches and befriending mail clerks. He created a following as his story was recounted in many local newspapers.

Owney's travel destinations have been recorded by the collection of leather and metal bagging tags, which were clipped to his collar and later to a harness-like jacket. The little traveler collected over one thousand tags and medals that were preserved by the Albany Post Office. Owney became both a national and international celebrity. He was a guest at business and political conventions, received awards at important dog shows, and even traveled around the world on a steamship. His journey included ports-of-call in China and Japan.

Mail clerks also considered Owney a good-luck charm. Accidents were frequent occurrences in the Railway Mail Service. However, there was never a derailment, collision, or explosion on a train that carried Owney as a passenger.

OWNEY

now wears big bunch [of tags]. When he jogs along, jingle like the bells on a junk wagon.

Owney, a stray mutt, wandered into the Albany, New York, post office in 1888. He fell asleep on some mailbags, and the clerks let him stay. Owney soon was riding mailbags across the country with the Railway Mail Service. In 1895, he traveled with mailbags on steamships to Asia and across Europe.

RMS clerks adopted Owney as their mascot, and began to record the dog's travels with medals and [attach]ed to his collar. Postmaster General John [...] was one of the pooch's fans. When he [...] dog's collar was weighed down by [... gave] Owney a jacket to display

Photo by Author

Owney at the National Postal Museum Washington, D.C.

In 1897, Owney's age and failing health sent him into involuntary retirement at the Albany Post Office where he began his career. But in June of that year, he slipped onto an Ohio-bound train for his final rail trip. He bit a postal worker after being mistreated and a gunshot ended his life.

Owney's many friends in the Railway Mail Service wanted his memory to live on. They collected enough money to have him preserved by a taxidermist in Toledo, Ohio. Since that time, Owney has been exhibited so that his story could be told. He was displayed with his impressive collection of medals and tags in St. Louis at the 1904 World's Fair as part of the United States Government's exhibit. In 1911, he was donated to the Smithsonian Institution. Today he can be seen at the National Postal Museum in Washington, D.C. His image is even depicted on the postmark printed on cards and letters sent from the museum, and also in a bronze sculpture at the entrance. Owney's fascinating story and legacy continue to live on today.

Photo by Author

Bronze Owney at entrance to National Postal Museum

Clear the Way —Snagboat Horatio G. Wright

A model of the Horatio G. Wright, a Mississippi River snagboat used by the U.S. Department of War 1904 World's Fair

The purchase of the Louisiana Territory ensured that the Port of New Orleans and the Mississippi River, the critical artery for western shipping and commerce, would be controlled by the United States. As traffic increased on this major waterway in the nineteenth century, it was essential that obstructions that would delay transit or destroy the boats and steamships be removed. This formidable task became one of the major missions of the federal government's Corps of Engineers. Continuously seeking better methods to clear the waterways of navigation obstacles, the Corps successfully employed new innovations, including steam-powered snagboats.

At the fair, the Corps of Engineers, then part of the U. S. Department of War, displayed a model of one of these powerful snagboats, the Horatio G. Wright. The actual boat was built in Carondelet near St. Louis in 1880 by the Western Iron Boat Building Company. The Wright had a heavy, v-shaped beam connecting its twin hulls that was used to ram and to release river snags. It also was equipped with powerful lifting machinery that was geared to its steam-powered engine. The Wright operated on the middle and lower Mississippi until it was decommissioned in 1941.

Two members of the Wright's crew built the model for viewing at the fair. After closing day, the model boat was exhibited in Philadelphia, at Chicago's Museum of Science and Industry, and on the West Coast. In 1980, it was returned to St. Louis after being on display in the Corps' Rock Island District Headquarters. Today the model can be seen at the National Mississippi River Museum and Aquarium on the banks of the Mississippi in Dubuque, Iowa.

The Wright riverboat model
National Mississippi River Museum and Aquarium in Dubuque, Iowa

Still Shining

Fit for Royalty — Prince Pu Lun Coach

(Bennitt/1904 LPE CD) Philip Geerling

Notable among the distinguished guests who visited the fair was Prince Pu Lun, nephew of the ruling emperor of China. During his two-month visit to St. Louis, foreign and state dignitaries, as well as exposition officials, honored the prince with receptions, social functions, and the trappings befitting royalty. In this vein, Adolphus Busch Sr., St. Louis beer brewer and fair promoter, provided a stately carriage for the young prince's driving and riding pleasure. Drawn by four horses, the prince was frequently seen with his attendants in this splendid, jet-black conveyance.

The C-Spring Victoria carriage was built in Rochester, New York, in 1880. The ornate brass lamps featured on the front of the vehicle burned oil rather than candles.

Today, this historic carriage is displayed in the Coach Room of the Bauernhof complex at the Anheuser-Busch Grant's Farm attraction in St. Louis. It is part of one of the most prized collections of coaches and carriages in the world.

Photo by Yvonne Suess

Prince Pu Lun of China (top)
C-Spring Victoria Carriage (bottom)
St. Louis, Missouri

The Book of the Fair, Ronald E. Schira Collection

Prince Pu Lun's coach
1904 World's Fair

Still Shining

Foreign Lights – French and Belgian Chandeliers

A building without windows, the Belgian Pavilion included hopvine chandeliers in a unique, filigree design to illuminate the interior space. To complement its lavish decor, the French Pavilion lit its displays with elegant chandeliers emblazoned with eagles. The massive light fixtures of these two foreign pavilions at the fair must have caught the eye of corporate beer-brewing giant Adolphus Busch.

**French Pavilion
1904 World's Fair**

The elaborate bronze tendrils of the Belgian hopvine fixtures may have been intriguing to Busch. Hops were depicted on the twin French chandeliers also, but it may have been the eagle insignias, quite similar to the famous brewery logo, that were most appealing. After the fair, Busch acquired these elegant yet functional pieces for installation in his business interests.

The pair of French chandeliers was subsequently separated. One

was installed in the opulent horse stable built on brewery property in St. Louis in 1885. Busch must have considered it an appropriate addition to the luxurious stables, which were adorned with hardwood paneling, enameled brick wainscoting, marble basins, and stained glass windows.

A permanent home for the second eagle-emblazoned chandelier was delayed until 1912 when Busch completed construction of a luxury hotel, the Aldolphus, in Dallas, Texas. His interest in the finest in arts and craftsmanship was reflected in the decor of the hotel and perhaps epitomized by

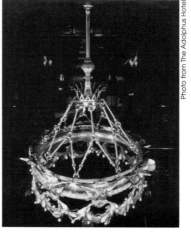

**French Pavilion chandeliers
Anheuser-Busch Horse Stable
(above) in St. Louis, Missouri, and
Adolphus Hotel (left) in
Dallas, Texas**

the inclusion of the second French chandelier in the hotel lobby. The hotel was renovated in 1980 to reflect its former grandeur. It has been placed on the National Register of Historic Places. The historic chandelier still lights the way for hotel guests.

The graceful hopvine chandelier from the Belgian Pavilion was installed in the atrium of the Anheuser-Busch Brew House in St. Louis to shine upon the brewers as they practiced their art.

Belgian Pavilion, 1904 World's Fair
The building was later moved to the Anheuser-Busch Brewery and used as the plant's glass works. It has since been razed.

Belgian Pavilion hopvine chandelier
Brew House, Anheuser-Busch Brewery
St. Louis, Missouri

Top of the Line — Gorham Martelé Silver

American manufacturers capitalized on the exposition to showcase their latest products to the thousands of visitors who browsed the exhibits daily. Leading-edge design and outstanding craftsmanship marked the Gorham Manufacturing Company's display of hand-wrought silver.

Martelé Centerpiece "Toilers of the Sea" 1904 World's Fair

At the end of the nineteenth century, Gorham's success as a mass producer of silverwares afforded the opportunity to revert to the creation of artistic pieces entirely by hand. Resulting from this endeavor was an exquisite art line of silver hollow-ware that carried the name Martelé, meaning hammered or hand-hammered. William C. Codman, Gorham's chief designer from 1891 to 1914, developed the acclaimed Martelé silverware. Designs were curvilinear in the art nouveau style. Each Martelé masterpiece was characterized by innovation in style and superlative hand-craftsmanship. Pieces were further distinguished as the design and execution were accomplished by the same person or in a close collaborative effort for a unified result.

Introduced at the Paris Exposition Universelle in 1900, Gorham's Martelé line dominated the prizes in St. Louis. The company was awarded the grand prize in the category for silversmith's and goldsmith's wares. Later, the beauty, originality, and prized-quality of the highly styled Martelé attracted notable purchasers including William Randolph Hearst and Helena Rubenstein.

Gorham lady's writing desk, Rhode Island School of Design Providence, Rhode Island

The Cincinnati Art Museum owns the exquisite boat-shaped punch bowl of hand-wrought silver that was displayed at the 1904 fair. This masterpiece incorporates mythological figures of Neptune and Venus, as well as mermaids and mermen into the graceful design.

The Gorham Manufacturing Company was founded in 1831 in Providence, Rhode Island. Interpreting the state's artistic heritage, the Rhode Island School of Design, also of Providence, holds the Gorham lady's writing desk, originally designed for the Department of Art in the American Section at the 1904 fair. This ebony furnishing with silver-gilt embellishment was fashioned with other fine materials including redwood, boxwood, mother-of-pearl, and ivory. Art nouveau floral motifs are abundant on the piece. The table desk, with its accompanying chair and writing set, received the grand prize for beauty and excellence in craftsmanship.

Still Shining

Golden Fossil of the Fair – Gingko Tree

Photo by Author

One living fossil from the fair literally had its roots there. As the story goes, ginkgo tree saplings were sold by Japanese exhibitors as souvenirs. One fairgoer bought one of those young trees and brought it back to Moberly, Missouri, as a gift to a neighbor. The sapling took root and today its trunk measures over 139 inches in circumference; three adults with outstretched arms can encircle the tree. Its lofty branches tower above the neighborhood. It's not surprising that the tree has flourished, as ginkgoes grow under almost any condition. This spectacular tree has even been admitted as a specimen of the International Golden Fossil Tree Society, which recognizes ginkgoes of special merit.

During the July 4, 1995, tornado in Moberly, the stately ginkgo held its ground as the storm passed within yards of its boughs; it suffered only minor damage. It stands on the lawn in front of a residence on South Williams Street.

Photo by Barbara Uhl

**Giant Gingko tree
Moberly, Missouri**

Max Storm Collection

THE JAPAN EXHIBIT ASSOCIATION
FOR THE L. P. E., 1904.

ST. LOUIS, MO., *Nov 15* 1904.

We are prepared to deliver you, on presentation of this card and the receipt at the Japanese Section, *F. F. & G.* Building, World's Fair, during the week ending the _____ day, the article described hereunder, which you had purchased of us, and, should the same be not taken delivery of before the date mentioned, it will be forwarded to you by express (C. O. D.) unless otherwise ordered. Respectfully yours,

VOUCHER NO. *4135*   DATE SOLD *Aug 20*

Quan.	Article	Exhibit No.	Balance Due	Exhibitor
	Ginko bamboo	*14*		

Will Call cards were issued for purchases of plant goods at the Palace of Forest, Fisheries and Game

Big Time – The Floral Clock

Billed as the largest timepiece in the world, the Great Floral Clock marked the passing hours on the gentle slope in front of the Palace of Agriculture. With a diameter that stretched 112 feet, the central portion of the dial was arrayed with verbenas. Fifteen-foot numerals marked the hours. Each was planted with colorful coleus. The outer rim of the dial reportedly featured "hour gardens," flowers that bloomed during certain hours of the day. At night, the clock was lit with one thousand lights concealed among the plantings.

**The Great Floral Clock
Palace of Agriculture, 1904 World's Fair**

(RauJ, Author)

The steel hands, each weighing 2,500 pounds, were driven by a master clock housed in the middle of three small pavilions at the top of the dial. Built by the Johnson Service Company of Milwaukee, Wisconsin, the mechanism regulated the release of compressed air into a piston that rapidly, yet precisely, moved the minute hand five feet every sixty seconds. On the hour, the doors of the central pavilion opened to show the splendid brass clock works that stood five and a half feet tall. A globe was also visible that gave the correct time of any place in the world. On the hour, a large hourglass turned in one of the two enclosures adjacent to the center clock pavilion while a 7,000-pound bell tolled on the hour and half-hour in the other. The clock operated from 8:00 a.m. to 8:00 p.m. daily.

At the close of the fair, the sleek master clock, resembling a grandfather clock, was placed in storage by the Johnson Service Company (known today as Johnson Controls). In 1939, the clock-works were acquired by William Schwanke of

Milwaukee's Schwanke-Kasten Jewelry Company. When the jewelry business was sold in 1958, the clock was included in the purchase. For years, it passed the hours in the Wells Building in downtown Milwaukee.

The 1904 World's Fair Society of St. Louis raised $20,000 to bring the 600-pound timepiece back to St. Louis in 1992. The historic master clock now resides near its original roots at the Missouri History Museum, located at the site of the main entrance to the historic fairgrounds.

Master clockworks (highlighted) in center pavilion
1904 World's Fair

Master clockworks
Missouri History Museum
St. Louis, Missouri

Still the Grandest – World's Largest Pipe Organ

Festival Hall, 1904 World's Fair

Festival Hall, the crown jewel of the fair, welcomed audiences to its 3,500-seat auditorium to experience memorable concerts and recitals on the world's largest pipe organ. Built by the Los Angeles Art Organ Company at a cost of $105,000, the musical masterpiece containing 10,059 pipes and 140 stops could produce an incredible 17,179,868,183 distinct tonal combinations. Renowned organists of the world, including the famous Parisian artist, Alexander Guilmant, performed dozens of concerts on the great organ.

As the music faded at the close of the fair, the mighty organ was slated for relocation to Kansas City, Missouri, but plans fell through. Relegated to a warehouse, it was not until 1909 that John Wanamaker purchased the organ to create a music center in the Grand Court of his Philadelphia department store. Transported from St. Louis on thirteen railroad cars, the organ was rebuilt in two years. On June 22, 1911, the John Wanamaker department store hosted the premiere performance of the reinstalled organ to coincide with the coronation of England's King George V.

The largest concert organ in the world, however, was not large enough to fill the Grand Court. By 1914, workers completed the installation of 8,000 additional pipes. In later years, a sixth keyboard was added. By 1930, the organ resonated through 30,000 pipes controlled by 451 stops. The expansion resulted in an instrument of great tonal quality

Great Organ — Festival Hall
Alexander Guilmant (left)

Still Shining

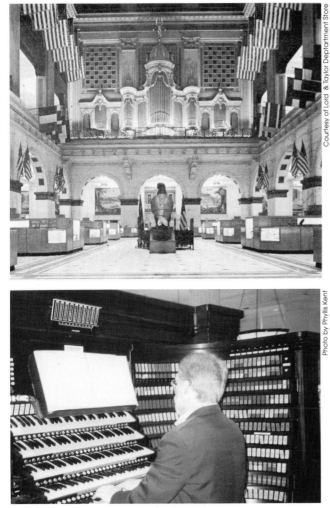

**Great Organ
Lord & Taylor Department Store
(formerly Wanamaker's)
Philadelphia, Pennsylvania**

and an incredible range of component sizes. The organ pipework is capable of producing the symphonic sound of three orchestras. With the smallest pipe a mere quarter-inch long, the largest pipe spans a length of thirty-two feet with interior dimensions once publicized by a photograph of a Shetland pony standing inside of it. The main console resides on the balcony above the store's main level; pipes are clustered in chambers throughout the multi-story atrium.

**Pony in largest
organ pipe**

For years, world-renowned organists gave after-hours concerts for the thousands that gathered as the store was transformed into a temporary music hall. Numerous choral groups, bands, guest artists, and even the Mormon Tabernacle Choir performed on the program with the magnificent organ. The store boasts that it has provided daily concerts for shoppers every business day since installation.

Over the years, the organ has required continuous maintenance. Parts of it have been extensively restored by skilled craftsmen who feel a sense of pride and honor to maintain this outstanding instrument.

Today, visitors and shoppers alike continue to flock to the store, now bearing the Lord & Taylor name, to enjoy midday concerts. The annual Christmas Light Show has delighted young and old with holiday lights and music from the great organ. Recognized as the grandest organ in the world today, its core is the instrument that was designed for the grandest of fairs. Valued now at over $50 million, this American musical treasure has been designated a National Historic Landmark.

A Life for Others — St. Elizabeth Mosaics

The sanctuary of St. Elizabeth of Hungary Church on Sappington Road in Crestwood, Missouri, is flanked by mosaic story panels created for the 1904 St. Louis World's Fair.

The two semi-circular mosaics were commissioned by the Busch family of St. Louis. Each is richly colored with gold accents in the Byzantine style and approximately ten-feet long. They were created by August Ortken and collaborators in Munich. Reportedly, Paul Heuduck, a young mosaicist, was involved in executing the work. Heuduck later immigrated to St. Louis to begin the project to create the now world-famous mosaic collection at the Cathedral Basilica of St. Louis and subsequently bought the Ravenna Mosaic Company that accomplished the work. At the fair, the panels were exhibited in the German Section of the Palace of Varied Industries. The exquisite murals portray the youthful betrothal and wedding of St. Elizabeth of Hungary. In 1906, the mosaics were donated to the St. Louis Art Museum and installed as arches over the entrances. They were frequently loaned for inclusion in exhibitions across the country. The two murals were subsequently offered to the Archdiocese of St. Louis. In 1962, both pieces were presented by Cardinal Joseph Ritter to the newly established St. Elizabeth parish in suburban St. Louis.

St. Elizabeth (1207-1231) was born to Hungarian royalty, but as she grew in piety she began to live a simple, austere life. A champion and patron of the poor, she spent the last years of her short life caring for the sick and establishing a hospital at Marburg. Perhaps it was the inspiration of this virtuous saint that led the Busch family to select her as the subject of the commissioned work.

The Offer of Marriage

**St. Elizabeth of Hungary Church
Crestwood, Missouri**

The Symbolic Wedding

Still Shining

The Solitary Column — Minnesota Shaft

Photo by Author

**Minnesota Shaft Monument
Park Lawn Cemetery
South St. Louis County, Missouri**

A huge granite column marks the gravesites of members of the St. Louis Typographical Union Number 8 at the Park Lawn Cemetery in South St. Louis County. That monument was a gift from the Louisiana Purchase Exposition Company and the State of Minnesota.

During the fair, the large polished granite shaft highlighted Minnesota's prize-winning exhibit in the Mines and Metallurgy Building. Mark Bennitt, in his *History of the Louisiana Purchase Exposition,* offers this description, "A large granite column three feet in diameter and twenty feet high, brought from the State Capitol, and seven large faced stones, set in cement, showed the appearance of the stone when used in construction." At the conclusion of the fair, Minnesota presented the column to David R. Francis, president of the Louisiana Purchase Exposition Company, for use in Forest Park, but those plans never materialized.

David R. Francis represented the Exposition Company and the State of Minnesota when the column was dedicated at the Park Lawn Cemetery on May 17, 1914. His address acknowledged the efforts of the typographical workers in relation to the success of the fair, "It seems eminently fit that this organization whose work was so potential in making that exposition's success through giving to the people of the civilized world information as to the character, extent and purpose of the enterprise should be linked in some befitting manner with the International Exposition of 1904. No more appropriate disposition could be made of the Minnesota column."

Several thousand people attended the ceremony that was filmed by the "St. Louis Times Movie Review" to be shown at local theaters.

Ring Out Freedom – The Liberty Bell

From June 8 to November 16, 1904, one of the most beloved symbols of American freedom was displayed at the fair. The Liberty Bell, that rang out to announce the first public reading of the Declaration of Independence on July 8, 1776, made its first trip west of the Mississippi River in 1904. The bell had been viewed with interest and reverence at five previous expositions, and St. Louisans wanted to honor it, too.

In February 1904, the Exposition Company sent a request to the state of Pennsylvania for the Liberty Bell to be displayed at the fair. The Pennsylvania Commission to the Louisiana Purchase

**Liberty Bell on horse-drawn wagon
1904 World's Fair**

Exposition voted to allow local officials in Philadelphia make the decision. The Philadelphia Merchants and Travelers Association and the Philadelphia Chapter of the Daughters of the American Revolution opposed the request. Perhaps the petition signed by seventy-five thousand St. Louis school children persuaded local authorities to allow the bell to journey from its shrine at Independence Hall in Philadelphia to the people in America's heartland.

Seventy-five thousand St. Louis school children signed petitions to have the Liberty Bell brought to the 1904 World's Fair

The bell traveled across the country under the care of the Pennsylvania Railroad Company. Thousands of patriotic Americans viewed the old bell on its five-day journey to St. Louis atop a specially built flat-bed car pulled by the Liberty Bell Special. The Special made twenty-nine stops as it snaked westward on a route that passed through Pennsylvania, New York, Ohio, Indiana, Illinois, Wisconsin, Minnesota, Iowa, and Missouri.

Cat. 2369, Independence National Historical Park

HOW THE BELL TRAVELS.

The Liberty Bell traveled to St. Louis aboard a Pennsylvania Railroad Company car

Admiring crowds gave the bell a splendid welcome at the fair. The day of its arrival, June 8, was officially declared "Liberty Bell Day" by St. Louis Mayor, Rolla Wells. The *World's Fair Bulletin* describes the scene as the famous symbol was paraded through the fairgrounds: "Liberty Bell was rested on a float draped with American flags, surrounded by patriotic legends and flanked by white doves on four sides. The float was drawn by thirteen iron-gray horses, each representing a State of the original thirteen states."

During its stay at the fair, the bell awed visitors from its place in the rotunda of the Pennsylvania Building. Fair President David R. Francis promised that the bell would be returned to Philadelphia unharmed. Four special guards from the Philadelphia Police Department provided added insurance to President Francis' pledge. Mayor Wells remarked that the Liberty Bell would be the most cherished memory of the magnificent fair.

Today, the celebrated symbol of American freedom is enshrined in the Liberty Bell Center on Independence Mall in downtown Philadelphia.

Photo by Author

**The Liberty Bell
Philadelphia, Pennsylvania**

Author

**Liberty Bell
souvenir pin**

All That Sparkles – Libbey Cut Glass

Masterpieces of American cut glass dazzled fairgoers who visited the "Golden Pavilion" of the Mermod and Jaccard jewelry firm in the Palace of Varied Industries. The jeweler was the exclusive agent in St. Louis for the Libbey Glass Company that displayed a sparkling array of cut glass created by master craftsmen. At the beginning of the twentieth century, Libbey Glass gained acclaim for the quality of its glass and the superb craftsmanship of its cutters and engravers.

(Bennitt) Author

**Libbey Glass Exhibit
1904 World's Fair**

Several notable pieces were designed and executed by Libbey specifically for the fair. These included a twenty-four-inch punch bowl, said to be one of the largest pieces of cut glass in the world, and a set of matching cups. The cover of the April 30, 1904 issue of *Scientific American* (concurrent with the opening of the fair) showed a picture of a craftsman polishing the huge, fair-destined punch bowl. The magazine included a feature article about the Libbey Glass Company. The magnificent bowl in fleur-de-lis motif and twenty-three matching cups are now in the collection of the Toledo Museum of Art.

A ninety-piece lead glass goblet set, considered a masterpiece of American copper wheel engraving, was also displayed at the fair. The Corning Museum of Glass (Corning, New York) and the Toledo Museum of Art now share part of this set of fine glassware. Each place setting in this collection consisted of a water goblet, and champagne, claret, wine, cordial and crème de menthe glasses.

Toledo Museum of Art

**Libbey cut glass table (left) and punch
bowl and cups (right)
Toledo Museum of Art
Toledo, Ohio**

Even glass furniture was created. The exhibit featured an exquisite cut glass table. The intricate designs in the table top, pedestal, and base took the artisan three and a half months to cut. The Toledo Museum of Art holds that table in its collection today.

The magnificent Libbey Glass exhibit with its 1,800 items was awarded a Grand Prize by the Louisiana Purchase Exposition Company.

Still Shining

Native North Americans — Vancouver Island Community

Native North American tribesmen from Canada and the government reservations in the American West were brought to St. Louis as participants in the Department of Anthropology exhibit. Living in traditional dwellings, these descendants of the earliest Americans provided a look into tribal culture and ceremony. Their rituals were filled with symbolism and those symbols were represented in their ceremonial dress and trappings.

Kwakiutl and Clayoquot tribesmen from the Vancouver Island, British Columbia, encamped at the fair. Members wore traditional coats and headdresses as the occasion directed. As part of their cultural heritage, they brought totem poles that were carved and decorated by their communities with images that told stories, legends, or tribal histories. The totem poles served as memory aids for retelling tribal lore.

When the fair closed, the Field Museum of Natural History in Chicago acquired many items from the North American Indian exhibits, including the ceremonial capes and headdresses worn by the two Kwakiutl tribesmen (left). The man on the far left wears a shirt made of cedar bark with attached carvings representing the Thunderbird. The other tribesman's headdress and outfit depict the crest of a killer whale. The elaborate totem pole held by the Clayoquot man to the right is also in the Field Museum collection.

Kwakiutl tribesmen
1904 World's Fair

(Rau) Ronald E. Schira Collection

Clayoquot tribesman
1904 World's Fair

Highlighting the Past –
Japanese Garden Lanterns at Como Park

Serenity and harmony are reflected in the careful designs of Japanese gardens. Trees, shrubs, and ornamentation are subtly yet deliberately placed into the landscape to create a natural setting, often serving as an oasis in the midst of crowded urban areas.

The Japanese Imperial Garden at the 1904 World's Fair provided a peaceful escape for visitors from around the world who strolled along its winding paths on the gentle hillsides near the Great Observation Wheel. It was a tranquil retreat within the hustle and bustle of the lively fairgrounds.

At the conclusion of the fair, Dr. Rudolph Schiffman transported part of this serene setting to Como Park in St. Paul, Minnesota. He purchased "a rare and large collection" of trees, shrubs, and four white granite lanterns from the Japanese Commission of the Louisiana Purchase Exposition Company. In 1905, Dr. Schiffman presented this core collection to Como Park for the creation of a Japanese Tea Garden along Cosey Lake.

Apparently the garden's glory faded after several years. The adjacent lake was drained and the land was cleared for a golf course.

(Bennit/1904 LPE CD) Philip Geerling

**Japanese Imperial Garden
1904 World's Fair**

After years in oblivion, there was renewed interest in recreating the extinct garden. In 1979, the present Japanese Garden at Como Park was dedicated. St. Paul's sister city, Nagasaki, generously donated the garden design as a special gift to its American friends. Created in the *Sansui* garden style, the central focus is a small pond fed by a waterfall. The four lanterns from the fair were reinstalled to accent the simplicity and subtle beauty of the landscape. From 1990 to 1991, the garden was extensively renovated and today's Como-Ordway Japanese Memorial Garden remains a jewel in historic Como Park.

1904 lanterns
Como Park
St. Paul, Minnesota

Write Here — Presidential Desk

David R. Francis, his name was synonymous with the success and magnitude of the Louisiana Purchase Exposition. As president of the Exposition Company, he exemplified the true "spirit of St. Louis" in his dedication and determination to host the grandest fair ever. Having served as former mayor of St. Louis, governor of Missouri, and Secretary of the Interior, Francis was well prepared to lead the effort from start to finish. Directly involved in the plans and activities of the fair, he garnered funding, sought national and foreign exhibitors, oversaw construction efforts, entertained distinguished world visitors, presided at numerous special events, and was the honored guest when closing day was declared "David R. Francis Day." Under his driving force and leadership, the fair exceeded all expectations in grandeur and in proceeds. The final entries in the ledger revealed figures "in the black" — uncommon for world's fairs. Under Francis' resolve, St. Louis experienced a magical year that spawned a remarkable legacy that still fascinates and is still celebrated a century later.

Photo by Author

**David R. Francis' desk
Angel motif (right)
Cole Country Historical Society
Jefferson City, Missouri**

Photo by Author

David R. Francis directed activities at the fair from his hilltop office in the Administration Building, now Robert S. Brookings Hall on the Washington University campus.

A carved desk used by Francis during the fair was donated to the Cole Country Historical Society in Jefferson City, Missouri, by his grandson. This distinctive desk features angelic motifs carved into each curved leg. It remains in the collection of the Cole County Historical Museum located near the Missouri Governor's Mansion in Jefferson City.

Rescued — Missouri Suite of Furniture

Missouri, the host state of the 1904 fair, constructed an impressive building with a commanding view of the fair-grounds. Designed by fair architect, Isaac S. Taylor, it was situated on top of Government Hill at the eastern edge of the Plateau of States. After welcoming thousands of visitors to its air-cooled reception rooms and offices, the structure was devastated by fire on November 19, less than two weeks before closing day. The building was leveled and the World's Fair Pavilion, built in 1909-10 by the Louisiana Purchase Exposition Company as a gift to the city, now occupies that site.

Missouri Buildling
1904 World's Fair

(Official Photographic Co.) Ronald E. Schira Collection

Mark Bennitt's account of the fire in his *History of the Louisiana Purchase Exposition* reported that "a volunteer salvage corps of bystanders . . . rescued the ten thousand volumes of the library and a large amount of the fine furniture." Among the items saved from the destruction was a suite of formal French chairs and settees with frames gilt in gold-leaf.

Photo by Author

Photo by Author

Rescued furniture from Missouri Building
Governor's Mansion
Jefferson City, Missouri

Appropriately, these splendid remnants of the Missouri Building were relocated to the Governor's Mansion at the State Capitol in Jefferson City. In the 1984 restoration of the ballroom at the mansion, the furniture was reupholstered in rich Victorian red and gold damask fabric, and the gold-leaf finish was restored. Additional pieces were replicated from the original design. Now lining the walls of the third-floor ballroom, the set of historic furniture still welcomes visitors who celebrate in Missouri.

Monument to a Mayor – Obelisk from the Fair

At the New St. Marcus Cemetery in South St. Louis, the gravesite of Henry Ziegenhein, mayor of St. Louis from 1897 to 1901, and the adjacent Koenig family plot are marked by prominent headstones. Each towers over the two family grave plots with fifty burial sites that Ziegenhein and Koenig purchased. Reportedly, both of the large granite obelisks that now mark the gravesites were once exhibited at the 1904 World's Fair. They were acquired after the fair and creatively reused; the monuments are among the tallest in the cemetery, rising to the height of about thirty feet. Each family name is emblazoned on the pedestal along with simple ornamentation added by the skilled hand of the stonecutter.

**Ziegenhein and Koenig monuments
New St. Marcus Cemetery
St. Louis, Missouri**

Detail of decoration on Ziegenhein Monument

To Defend — Department of War Display

The United States government extensively supported the 1904 World's Fair, financing one-third of the start-up costs and appropriating nearly $1.5 million for the government exhibits, including those of the Alaskan and Indian territories. Displays from each executive department conveyed the great history of the country, demonstrated the latest scientific and medical achievements, and showcased other advancements to promote and protect the welfare of the nation.

The War Department ordnance display exhibited the latest methods of warfare and defense, including cannons, rifles, uniforms, and even "stuffed" horse and mule teams showing how guns and munitions were transported to field positions. The Army used horse mannequins (full hides mounted on plaster forms) to design and to fit artillery harness and cavalry equipment. Numerous handguns and rifles confiscated

**Artillery display (above)
1904 World's Fair**

**Nordenfelt-Kranz machine
gun today (right)
Rock Island Arsenal
Museum**

**Horse and mule
teams (above)
1904 World's Fair**

**Taxidermic horse
model (right)
Rock Island Arsenal
Museum**

during the Philippine Insurrection were also featured, including a British-made Nordenfelt-Kranz machine gun. The Rock Island Arsenal in northern Illinois sent a sizable collection for inclusion in the exhibit.

In 1903, the Rock Island Arsenal in northern Illinois was designated as the site for a Military Museum that opened in 1905. At the conclusion of the fair, the government retained many of the items including the full-size taxidermic horse models, a machine gun, and Philippine Insurrection weaponry. The items were set to Rock Island where selected pieces may be seen in the historical collection today.

A Visitor from the Jurassic Age – A Dinosaur at the Fair

The Smithsonian Institution provided an extensive display of taxidermic specimens, models, and skeletons of exotic and unusual creatures that roamed the earth from prehistoric times to the current day. The Department of Geology added a recreation of an extinct inhabitant of the American West to that collection with a papier-mache model of a Stegosaurus dinosaur.

Created by the Milwaukee Papier Mache Works in 1903, modelers worked with scientists at the Smithsonian to fabricate the full-scale reptile with its distinctive bony-plated spine and strong spiked tail. The twenty-foot long dinosaur stood twelve feet tall and weighed just five hundred pounds, but was strong enough to support the weight of two men. It was shipped to St. Louis for its debut appearance at the fair in the U.S. Government Building.

**Stegosaurus dinosaur model
National Museum of Natural History
Smithsonian Institution,
Washington D.C.**

(Stereoview: Underwood & Underwood) Yvonne Suess Collection

**Two views of
Stegosaurus
Dinosaur
U.S. Government
Building
1904 World's Fair**

(Bennitt) Author

Now a centenarian itself, the Stegosaurus continues to attract the attention of curious visitors to its home in Dinosaur Hall at the Smithsonian Institution's National Museum of Natural History in Washington, D.C.

1904 Olympian Games – Olympic Venues

S t. Louis was a national focal point in 1904. Besides hosting an international fair with millions of visitors from all corners of the world, St. Louis welcomed numerous organizations that scheduled meetings, conferences, and conventions in the city that year. St. Louis went for the gold, too, by securing rights to host the 1904 Olympic Games.

When the fair was pushed back from 1903 to a 1904 opening, the Exposition Company challenged the selection of Chicago as the host city for the 1904 Olympic Games. Fair officials met with Chicago Olympic organizers who decided to leave the decision up to the president of the International Olympic Committee, Pierre de Coubertin. He approved the transfer and St. Louis became the first American city to host the Olympics since their revival in 1896.

From the collection of Jim Greenstelder, Cincinnati, Ohio

**1904 Olympics
Participation Medal**

The Olympian Games of 1904, as they were called, were considered events of the World's Fair. They were administered under the Department of Physical Culture. But to confuse the issue, all related athletic competitions affiliated with the fair were also designated as Olympic events. From May through November, "Olympic" sporting events of all types were held, including scholastic competitions at all levels, gymnastics (turnverein), basketball, golf, rowing, boxing, tennis, bicycling, swimming, fencing, archery, wrestling, and football. Nevertheless, twenty-two "sanctioned" track and field events of the third modern Olympics were held between August 29 and September 3.

(Bennitt) Author

**Dumbbell competition
1904 Olympic Games
Athletic Field at
Washington University**

(Bennitt/1904 LPE CD) Philip Geerling

**1904 Olympic Games — 200 Meter Race
Athletic Field at Washington University**

The Olympics of 1904 lacked the structure and pageantry that have developed in the ensuing competitions. Athletes participated as members of an athletic club, college, or as independent competitors, not as part of organized national teams. Contestants from only eleven foreign nations participated with American athletes in those events now designated as the official Olympic competition of the St. Louis games. In the sanctioned track and field competition, the majority of the contenders were from the United States — 539 of the 687 total participants. An estimated nine thousand athletes competed in all of the sporting events throughout the run of the fair.

The St. Louis games introduced the tradition of awarding gold, silver, and bronze medals to the first, second, and third prize winners — a popular ceremonial tradition that has continued. The first African American Olympic contenders participated and medaled in the official two hundred-meter and four hundred-meter hurdles; standing high jump; and hop, step and jump competitions. Track and field competitors thrilled crowds in the first concrete and steel stadium ever built. That outdoor venue held fifteen thousand spectators and featured a one-third-mile cinder track with a two hundred-meter straight-away.

In the St. Louis area, several sites of the 1904 Olympic sporting events continue to serve athletes and sportsmen today. Glen Echo Country Club hosted the two golf competitions, the singles and team championships. Fifteen holes of the eighteen-hole course retain the 1904 configuration. Rowing competition, known as the Olympic Regatta of the National Association of Amateur Oarsmen (NAAO), was held at Creve Coeur Lake. Continuing a long tradition, the St. Louis Rowing Club still practices and competes at that popular recreation site. Currently, the lake is half the size it was in 1904.

First place team
Century Boat Club of St. Louis
Senior International four-oared shells
1904 Olympics

Rowers today
Creve Coeur Lake
St. Louis, Missouri

Historic Fairway at Hole 15 (The Lake)
retains the 1904 configuration.
Glen Echo Country Club
St. Louis, Missouri

Still Shining

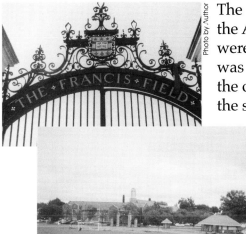

The twenty-two track and field events of the official Olympic competition were contested at the Athletic Field at Washington University in St. Louis. After the fair, the stadium and track were named in honor of World's Fair and 1904 Olympics President, David R. Francis, who was also an alumnus of the university. While the cinder track has been replaced, much of the original concrete grandstand is still intact although it has been resurfaced. Adjacent to the stadium, the Francis Gymnasium, called the Physical Culture Building during the fair and Olympic events, had complete facilities for basketball competition. It was fully equipped with an elevated running track, with workout apparatus and for aquatic exercise. Tennis, archery, and bicycling events also took place on the university grounds. A large historical marker on North and South Road at Shaftesbury Avenue in University City, a St. Louis suburb, identifies part of the original route of the abbreviated Olympic marathon that began and ended at the Athletic Field. The course in the St. Louis games was just under twenty-five miles, a bit shorter than the regulation distance of twenty-six miles and 385 yards of today.

**Francis Field
Washington University
St. Louis, Missouri**

The 1904 Olympic Games and events take their place of distinction in St. Louis' proud and celebrated sports history.

**1904 Marathon Marker
University City, Missouri**

**Francis Gymnasium today
(interior and exterior)
Washington University**

In conclusion

"*I have but one regret, and that is a deep regret—the regret that these buildings and these exhibits could not be made permanent; that these buildings cannot be maintained as they are for our children and our children's children and all who are to come after, as a permanent memorial of the greatness of this country. I think that an American who begrudges a dollar that has been spent here is not so far-sighted as he should be. It is a credit to the United States to have had such an exposition carried on so successfully from the beginning to its conclusion.*"

Theodore Roosevelt
November 26, 1904

Legacies

At the close of the fair, St. Louisans realized their accomplishment. They had created a virtual kingdom within their city and became a world focus for seven fabulous months. St. Louis was now "on the map" and "on the move" as the success of the fair fueled the community's can-do spirit. The event provided a major boost toward the development and vitality of the city's cultural, civic, and academic communities, as well as improving its infrastructure. The 1904 Louisiana Purchase Exposition continues to touch the lives of St. Louisans today through the legacies left behind and the momentum it generated to build the future.

St. Louis Art Museum Building, Forest Park. The central portion of the Art Palace was a gift of the Exposition Company to the city.

St. Louis Zoo, Forest Park. The Flight Cage inspired the effort that led to the development of the world-renowned St. Louis Zoo.

Jefferson Memorial, Forest Park (1911-1913). Erected by the Exposition Company as a gift to the city, it stands on the site of the main entrance to the fairgrounds. The building is now home to the Missouri History Museum.

Washington University, St. Louis. Rental income from the fair for use of campus buildings averted the funding crisis that threatened the university's construction program for its new campus.

Statue of St. Louis, Forest Park, 1906. Originally made of staff (plaster and hemp mixture) at the fair, this popular sculpture was recast in bronze and erected on Art Hill in front of the Art Museum at the site of Festival Hall. It was presented by the Exposition Company as a gift to the city to commemorate the Universal Exposition of 1904. It has since been a symbol of the city.

World's Fair Pavilion, Forest Park (1909-1910). Erected on the site of the Missouri Building, it was a gift from the Exposition Company to the city. The pavilion now serves as a site for public events.

Painting and Sculpture (statuary), Forest Park (1913). Originally made of staff at the fair, these two statues were recreated in marble and flank the main entrance to the Art Museum.

The Muny, (St. Louis Municipal Opera, Forest Park (1919). The Muny, St. Louis' premiere outdoor theater, credits the 1904 fair for sparking the dream that led to its reality a decade and a half later.

Clean water supply. To ensure that the waters flowing over the Cascade Terraces beneath Festival Hall were crystal clear, the city re-engineered its water system that ultimately provided pure rather than murky water to residents.

The Grand Basin. At the foot of Art Hill in Forest Park, this expansive pool has been returned to its 1904 splendor with the reintroduction of elegant promenades, bridges, and fountains.

The fair generated new civic pride and gave the year '04 a special meaning in St. Louis, not only in cherished memories, but in the real "spirit of St. Louis" that it still inspires today.

Photo by Melanie Raffel

1904 World's Fair Pavilion today
Forest Park
St. Louis, Missouri

Treasures by State

State	City	Item
Alabama	Birmingham	Vulcan
Alaska	Sitka	Totem Poles
California	Atascadero	Water Nymphs
Illinois	Cahokia	Cahokia Courthouse
	Cairo	The Hewer
	Chicago	Vancouver Island Community artifacts
	Rock Island	Department of War exhibit
Indiana	West Lafayette	Connecticut State Pavilion
Iowa	Dubuque	Snagboat Wright Model
Kansas	Lindsborg	Swedish Homestead
Kentucky	Louisville	The Thinker
Missouri	Cape Girardeau	Gerber-Houck Statuary
	Columbia	Thomas Jefferson's Tombstone Monument
	Jefferson City	Missouri Pavilion furniture Presidential Desk Signing of the Treaty Statue
	Kansas City	Japanese Eagle Statue
	Moberly	Gingko Tree
	St. Louis	American Radiator Building Art Palace (including Statue of St. Louis, Painting and Sculpture) Belgium Pavilion Chandelier British Pavilion Chandeliers Flight Cage Floral Clockworks Florentine Singer Forest Devotion Fountain Angel French Pavilion Chandeliers General Grant's Cabin Japanese Lanterns

State	City	Item
Missouri	St. Louis	Japanese Vase Minnesota Shaft Nevada State Pavilion Obelisk Olympic Games Venues Press Building Prince Pu Lun Coach Rhode Island State Pavilion St. Elizabeth Mosaics Utah State Pavilion Von Steuben Statue Washington University Buildings Wisconsin State Pavilion
	Smithville	Apollo Statue
New York	Corning	Libbey Glass
	Monticello	Japanese Garden Buildings
	New York	The Mares of Diomedes
Ohio	Cincinnati	Gorham Silver
	Toledo	Libbey Glass
Oklahoma	El Reno	Oklahoma Territory Building
Pennsylvania	Philadelphia	Liberty Bell German Eagle World's Grandest Organ
Rhode Island	Providence	Gorham Silver
Texas	Austin	Gen. Albert Sidney Johnston Memorial Statue
	Dallas	French Pavilion Chandelier
Washington D.C.		Owney Stegosaurus

About the Author

Like many native St. Louisans, Diane Rademacher "inherited" an interest in the 1904 St. Louis World's Fair from her family. Her father, born in 1904, attended the fair as a baby with her grandparents, and a great uncle was a Louisiana Purchase Exposition stock-holder. With that connection, collecting fair history has been a lifelong avocation. Diane is a charter member of the 1904 World's Fair Society, founded in 1986.

Diane was born and raised in historic South St. Louis city. She holds a bachelor's degree in history with honors from the University of Missouri-St. Louis, where she has also done graduate work. She has written articles related to computer systems, and compiled and edited the centennial history of her parish. Diane is a management analyst for the federal government.

Bibliography/Credits

BOOKS

The American Woman's Republic Founded by The American Woman's League. University City, MO, c 1911.

Amsler, Kevin. *Final Resting Place: The Lives and Deaths of Famous St. Louisans.* St. Louis: Virginia Publishing Company, 1997.

Baldwin, Helen I. *Heritage of St. Louis.* St. Louis: St. Louis Public Schools, 1964.

Bennitt, Mark, ed. *History of the Louisiana Purchase Exposition.* St Louis: Universal Exposition Publishing Company, 1905.

Benson, Sally. *Meet Me in St. Louis.* New York: Random House, 1941.

Billdt, Ruth Bergin and Elizabeth Jaderborg. *The Smoky Valley in the After Years* (contains article by Schon, Anders, *Sweden's House in St. Louis "Sveriges hus i St. Louis"* From Prairieblomman, p. 115). Lindsborg, KS: Lindsborg News-Record, 1969.

Birk, Dorothy Daniels. *The World Came to St. Louis: A Visit to the 1904 World's Fair.* St. Louis: The Bethany Press, 1979.

Buel, J.W., ed. *Louisiana and the Fair: An Exposition of the World, Its People and Their Achievements.* 10 vols. St. Louis: World's Progress Publishing Co., 1904-1905.

Bruns, James (text compiled by). *Owney: Mascot of the Railway Mail Service.* A Publication of the National Postal Museum, Smithsonian Institution, Washington, D.C.: Kisel Printing Inc., 1990 (revised 1992).

Carter, Robin Borglum. *Gutzon Borglum: His Life and Work.* Austin, TX: Eakin Press, 1998.

The City Art Museum of St. Louis: Handbook of the Collections. St. Louis: Buxton & Skinner, Printers, 1953.

Clevenger, Martha R. *"Indescribably Grand": Diaries and Letters from the 1904 World's Fair.* St. Louis: Missouri Historical Society Press, 1996.

Cole, Douglas. *Captured Heritage: The Scramble for Northwest Coast Artifacts.* Seattle: University of Washington Press, 1985.

Corrigan, Patricia. *Wild Things: Untold Tales from the First Century of the Saint Louis Zoo.* St. Louis: Virginia Publishing Company, 2002.

Conway, Freeman R., ed. *Report of the Iowa Commission to the Louisiana Purchase Exposition, St. Louis, 1904.* Des Moines, IA: The Register and Leader Company, 1905?

Coyle, Elinor Martineau. *Old St. Louis Homes, 1764-1865: The Stories They Tell,* St. Louis: Folkestone Press, 1979.

Cutrer, Emily Fourmy. *The Art of the Woman: The Life and Work of Elisabet Ney.* Lincoln, NE: University of Nebraska Press, 1988.

Earngey, Bill. *Missouri Roadsides: The Traveler's Companion.* Columbia, MO: University of Missouri Press, 1995.

Elsen, Albert Edward. *Rodin's Thinker and the Dilemmas of Modern Public Sculpture.* New Haven: Yale University Press, c1985.

Everett, Marshall. *The Book of the Fair.* Philadelphia: P. W. Ziegler Co., 1904.

Fauster, Carl U. *Libbey Glass Since 1818: Pictorial History & Collector's Guide.* Toledo, OH: Len Beach Press, 1979.

Fox, Tim, ed. *Where We Live, A Guide to St. Louis Communities.* St. Louis: Missouri Historical Society Press, 1995.

Fox, Timothy J. and Duane R. Sneddeker. *From the Palaces to the Pike: Visions of the 1904 World's Fair.* St. Louis: Missouri Historical Society Press, 1997.

Francis, David R. *The Universal Exposition of 1904.* 2 vols. St. Louis: Louisiana Purchase Company, 1913.

The Greatest of Expositions. St. Louis: Official Photographic Company, 1904.

Greensfelder, Jim, and Jim Lally, Bob Christianson and Max Storm. *1904 Olympic Games, St. Louis, Missouri.* Cincinnati, OH and Saratoga, CA: GVL Enterprises, 2001.

Griffin, Kristen. *Early Views: Historical Vignettes of Sitka National Historical Park.* Anchorage: Alaska Support Office, National Park Service and Sitka National Historic Park, 2000.

Halstead, Murat. *Pictorial History of the Louisiana Purchase and the World's Fair at St. Louis.* Philadelphia: Frank S. Brant, 1904.

Hardy, Hugh, and Malcolm Holzman, Norman Pfeiffer and James N. Wood. *The Architecture of the St. Louis Art Museum 1904–1977.* St. Louis: Sayers Printing Company, 1978.

Harris, Nini. *Legacy of Lions.* University City, MO: The Historical Society of University City, 1981.

Hilton, Suzanne. *Here Today and Gone Tomorrow: The Story of World's Fairs and Expositions.* Philadelphia: The Westminster Press, 1978.

Ives, Halsey C., and Charles M. Kurtz and George Julian Zolnay. *Official Illustrations of Selected Works in the Various National Sections of the Department of Art.* St. Louis: Louisiana Purchase Exposition Company for the Official Catalogue Company, 1904. (Also referenced as *The Art Department Illustrated.*)

Jackson, C. S. *Jackson's Famous Photographs of the Louisiana Purchase Exposition.* Chicago: Metropolitan Syndicate Press, 1904.

Jaderborg, Elizabeth. *Why Lindsborg?* Lindsborg, KS: Lindsborg News-Record, 1976.

Keefe, John Webster and Samuel J. Hough. *Magnificent, Marvelous Martelé: American Art Nouveau Silver: The Jolie and Robert Shelton Collection.* New Orleans, LA: New Orleans Museum of Art, 2001.

Kelsay, Lillie F. *Historic and Dedicatory Monuments of Kansas City.* Kansas City, MO: Kansas City Missouri Board of Parks and Recreation Commissioners, 1987.

Kimbrough, Mary. *The Muny: St. Louis' Outdoor Theater.* St. Louis: The Bethany Press, 1978.

Kirtz, Mary Jane. *Sculpture, Fountains, Pools and Ponds at Missouri Botani-*

Still Shining

cal Garden. St. Louis: Missouri Botanical Garden, 1988.

Lancaster, Clay. The Japanese Influence in America. New York: Abbeville Press, 1983.

Lewis, William H. Atascadero's Colony Days. Atascadero, CA: The Treasure of El Camino Real (The Atascadero Historical Society), 1974.

Loughlin, Caroline, and Catherine Anderson. Forest Park. Columbia, MO: The Junior League of St. Louis and University of Missouri Press, 1986.

Lowmiller, America, and Florence Logan, Carl Massie, Francis Williams and Link V. Evans. Progress-a-Rama: History of Smithville. Smithville, MO: B&B Printing, 1967.

Martin, John H. (ed.). Journal of Glass Studies, Vol XIX, Corning, NY: The Corning Museum of Glass, 1977 contains article Libbey Cut Glass Exhibit, St. Louis World's Fair, 1904 by Carl U. Fauster (p. 160).

Mattingly, Arthur H. Normal to University: A Century of Service. Cape Girardeau, MO: Southeast Missouri State University, 1979.

McCue, George. Sculpture at the Missouri Botanical Garden. St. Louis: Kohler and Sons, Inc., 1988.

McCue, George. Sculpture City, St. Louis: Public Sculpture in the "Gateway to the West." New York: Hudson Hills Press, Inc., 1988.

McCue, George and Frank Peters. A Guide to the Architecture of St. Louis. Columbia, MO: University of Missouri Press, 1989.

Memories of the Louisiana Purchase Exposition. Grand Rapids, MI: James Bayne Company, 1904.

Monkhouse, Christopher P. American Furniture in Pendleton House. Providence, RI: Museum of Art, Rhode Island School of Design, 1986.

Morris, Ann. Sacred Green Space: A Survey of Cemeteries in St. Louis County. St. Louis, MO: s.n., 2000.

Morrow, Ralph E. Washington University in St. Louis: A History. St. Louis: Missouri Historical Society Press, 1996.

Official Guide to the Louisiana Purchase Exposition. St. Louis: The Official Guide Co., 1904.

Official Louisiana Purchase Exposition, Official Photographers. St. Louis: The Official Photographic Co., 1904.

Paige, John C. The Liberty Bell of Independence National Historical Park: A Special History Study. Denver, CO: Denver Service Center, National Park Service, United States Department of the Interior, 1985.

Peden, William. The Jefferson Monument at the University of Missouri. Columbia, MO: University of Missouri Press, 1976.

Peters, Laura, ed. The Muny: A History of the People Who Have Made and Kept the Muny . . . Alone In Its Greatness, 1993.

Pickard, John. Report of the Capitol Decoration Commission. Columbia, MO: 1928.

Pickens, Buford and Margaretta J. Darnell. Washington University in St. Louis, Its Design and Architecture. St. Louis: School of Architecture, Washington University, 1978.

Portfolio of Photographs of the World's Fair: St. Louis, 1904. Chicago: The Educational Company, 1904.

Primm, James Neal. Lion of the Valley: St. Louis, Missouri. Boulder, CO: Pruett Publishing Company, 1990 (2nd ed.).

Report of the Board of Lady Managers St. Louis 1904. Board of Lady Managers Louisiana Purchase Exposition, 1905.

The Rhode Island Building. Published by the Rhode Island Commission, 1904.

Smith, Joanne. The Adolphus Cookbook. Dallas, TX: Taylor Publishing Company, c1983.

Spielman, Sir Isadore. Royal Commission, St. Louis International Exhibition, 1904: The British Section. London: The Royal Commission, 1906.

A Souvenir of the St. Louis and the Louisiana Purchase Exposition. Grand Rapids, MI: James Bayne Co., 1904.

The St. Louis Art Museum, Handbook of the Collections. Japan: Toppan Printing Company, 1991.

The St. Louis Exposition 1904. Philadelphia: J. Murray Jordan, 1904.

Spillman, Jane Shadel. Glass From World's Fairs, 1851-1904. Corning, NY: Corning Museum of Glass, 1986.

Taylor, Mrs. Howard and Mrs. Harold Harris. Notes from Yesterday. Kearney, MO: Published/printed by Whipple, 1966.

Travis, Marguerite A. The Birth of Atascadero. Atascadero, CA: Atascadero Historical Society, 1989 (3rd Printing).

Vulcan & His Times. Birmingham: Birmingham Historical Society (Publishers), 1995.

Way, Frederick, Jr. Way's Packet Directory 1848-1983: Passenger Steamboats of the Mississippi River System Since the Advent of Photography in Mid-Continent America. Athens, OH: Ohio University, 1983.

Wayman, Norbury L. History of St. Louis Neighborhoods: Kingsbury. St. Louis: St. Louis Community Development Agency, 1978.

White, Marjorie Longenecker. The Birmingham District: An Industrial History and Guide. Birmingham, AL: Birmingham Publishing Company, 1981.

Witherspoon, Margaret Johanson. Remembering the St. Louis World's Fair. St. Louis: Comfort Printing Co., 1973.

World's Fair Authentic Guide. St. Louis: The Official Guide Co., 1904.

The World's Fair Comprising The Official Photographic Views of the Universal Exposition Held in Saint Louis, 1904. The Official Photographic Company, William H. Rau (Managing Director). St. Louis: N. D. Thompson Publishing Company, 1903 (1904).

PERIODICALS

Adams, Joni. "Statuary Hall Lives Again!" Alumni Signal (October 1978), pp. 8-9. (Reprinted article from the Bulletin-Journal, a Cape Girardeau, MO, newspaper).

Ban, Ericka. "Paradise Found." Where St. Louis. (May 1999), pp. 16-18.

DeBellis, Steven J., ed. "Busch Funeral Today." St. Louis Inquirer 4:2 (February 1989), p. 5.

"Entrance Garden Named for Harrises." (caption) Missouri Botanical Garden Bulletin 87 (September/October 1999), p. 12.

Flint, Edward W. "An Unknown American Organ Builder: William Boone Fleming." The Stentor (Newsletter of Friends of the Wanamaker Organ) 1:2 (Winter 1993), pp. 6-8.

"4 'State Houses' Remain From the World's Fair." *St. Louis Home/Garden* (March 1979), pp. 14-15 and 52-53.

"Gift of Libbey Stemware Made for St. Louis World's Fair." *Hobbies — The Magazine for Collectors* (September 1969), p. 130.

Gill, Brendan. "Imperial Retreat, A Replica of Kyoto's Eleventh-Century Palace in Upstate New York." *Architectural Digest* 51:12 (December 1994), pp. 134-141.

"Holiday Show Gets New Curtain." *The Stentor* (Newsletter of Friends of the Wanamaker Organ) 1:2 (Winter 1993), p. 3.

Iglauer, Henry S. "The Demolition of the Louisiana Purchase Exposition of 1904." *Missouri Historical Society Bulletin* 22. (July 1966), pp. 457-467.

"The Jefferson Monument." *The University of Missouri Bulletin* 33:13 (General Series 1932).

Jensen, Billie Snell. "St. Louis Celebrates." *Missouri Historical Society Bulletin* 11 (October 1954), pp.54-72.

Lancaster, David, ed. *Lewis and Clark In St. Louis, the Complete Story of the Corps of Discovery in the St. Louis Area: Cahokia, St. Louis, Camp River Dubois, St. Charles, Fort Bellefontaine.* St. Louis Family 2003 published by WHERE St. Louis.

"Lanterns Shed 1904 Light on Japanese Garden History." *Missouri Botanical Garden Bulletin* 64:11 (November 1976), p. 4.

"The Liberty Bell Welcomed to the World's Fair by 75,000 Children." *The World's Fair Bulletin* (July 1904), pp. 2-4.

"Liberty Bell, Returned to Philadelphia from World's Fair." *The World's Fair Bulletin* (December 1904), p. 24.

McKenzie, Molly. "Reconstructing the Cahokia Courthouse." *Historic Illinois* 7:1 (June 1984), pp. 8-11.

"Missouri Dealer Offers Wide Array of St. Louis World's Fair Mementoes." *The Stentor* (Newsletter of Friends of the Wanamaker Organ) 4:1 (Spring 1995), p. 8.

"Restoring the Many Records of the Louisiana Purchase." *NARA Staff Bulletin* 516 (April 2003), p. 1 [exerpted from "Jefferson Buys Louisiana Territory and the Nation Moves Westward," by Wayne De Cesar and Susan Page, *Prologue* (Spring 2003)].

1904 World's Fair Swedish Pavilion Restoration Project 1:1 (January 1999), pp. 1-6 and 1:2 (July 1999) pp. 1-6.

O'Brien, Frank. "Meet Me in St. Louis." *Washington University Magazine* (Spring 1974), pp. 7-13.

Official List of Concessionaires. *The World's Fair Bulletin.* (April 1904), pp. 41-43.

Peterson, Charles E. "Notes on Old Cahokia." *Journal of the Illinois State Historical Society* 42:3 (September 1949), p. 330.

Provenzo, Eugene F. Jr. "Education and The Louisiana Purchase Exposition." *Missouri Historical Society Bulletin* 32 (January 1976), pp. 99-109.

Simon, John Y. (with an introduction by Paul Siemer). "The House That Grant Built, Hardscrabble." *Missouri Life* (May-August 1979) pp. 34-37.

Stewart, John P. "misc file." *St. Louis Commerce* (March 1983), p. 16.

Storm, Max. "The Greatest Exhibition of Them All." *Nostalgia Magazine* (July / August 1988), pp. 4-10.

"Universal Exposition of 1904, The Division of Exhibits." *The World's Fair Bulletin* (1904).

Valhalla Mausoleum (advertisement), *The Greater St. Louis Magazine* 6:6 (December 1968), p. 38.

Van der Spek, Peter. "Restoration Update." *The Stentor* (Newsletter of Friends of the Wanamaker Organ) 4:1 (Spring 1995), p. 5.

Walker, John Brisben. "The World's Fair." *The Cosmopolitan* 37:5 (September 1904).

"When the Smoke Cleared: The Louisiana Purchase Exposition Came to Webster Groves." *Retrospect III* (1978), Webster Groves Senior High School, Webster Groves, MO, pp. 6-13.

Whiting, Marvin Y., ed. "Giuseppe Moretti." *The Journal of the Birmingham Historical Society* 9:1 (December 1985).

NEWSPAPERS

Cairo Bulletin (Illinois)
  October 26, 1904.
Cairo Evening Citizen (Illinois)
  October 5, 1966. The Hewer Remains Priceless Art Treasure and Tourist Attraction (no author).
Cape Girardeau Southeast Missourian
  September 14, 1975. Statuary Hall No More; SEMO Replicas Scattered about Campus, Some Destroyed by Judith Ann Crow.
El Reno Globe (Oklahoma)
  August 19, 1904. Oklahoma Day.
The Courier Journal (Louisville, Kentucky)
  March 23, 1986. 'The Thinker' at the U of L sits tall among other casts of Rodin statue by Diane Heilenman.
Lafayette Journal and Courier (Indiana)
  September 3, 1994. 'A precious time' by Kevin Cullen.
  November 10, 2002. Home Sweet Home by Kevin Cullen.
Lindsborg News Record (Kansas)
  August 7, 1969. Early Frontier Holds Memories for Hagstrand.
  April 18, 1976. Thomas Was Responsible For Pavilion Coming to Lindsborg by Elizabeth Jaderborg.
  July 29, 1976. Relative of Pavilion Builder Visits Lindsborg.
Naborhood Link News (St. Louis, Missouri)
  November 27, 1991. Society Raising Funds to Purchase Great Floral Clock from 1904 Fair.
Salina Journal (Kansas)
  April 28, 1968. Old Swedish Pavilion May Again Display Swedish Arts by Mike Smith
South Side Journal (St. Louis Suburban Journals)
  November 18, 1992. Stately Utah House set for renovation by Lois Kendall.
St. Louis Globe Democrat
  April 22, 1979. 1904…when the world met at the fair by Mary Kimbrough.
  March 16, 1977. Rhode Island building at 1904 Fair has new role and location by Barney Wippold.
St. Louis Post Dispatch
  May 27, 1990. White Haven, A Hold on the Heart by Patricia Rice.
  October 27, 1991. Time To Remember: 'Flower Clock' From 1904 Fair May Bloom Again by Judith VandeWater.
  February 19, 1995. German Foundry's Ties To St. Louis by

Robert L. Koenig.
April 26, 1997. A Beautiful 'Living Fossil' by Patricia Corrigan
July 21, 1998. Our Treasures by John M. McGuire.

St. Louis Republic
December 4, 1904. World's Fair Palaces and Pavilions Sold for a Song, Though They Cost Millions.

St. Louis Times
May 18, 1914. Printers' Memorial Shaft is Unveiled.

Southwest County Sunday Home Journal (St. Louis, Missouri)
May 10, 1992. Matter of time, World's Fair Society seeks funding for floral clock by Lois Kendall.

Webster-Kirkwood Journal
July 3, 2002. City searches for its history by Robbi Courtaway.
July 3, 2002. Historic homes need touching up by Robbi Courtaway.

PAMPHLETS/BOOKLETS/FACT SHEETS

Auguste Rodin 1997 (calendar), Paris: Musée Rodin, 1995.

Birmingham's Vulcan world's largest iron man (brochure #150-8.94), Birmingham Park & Recreation Board, City of Birmingham.

A Brief History of John Wanamaker, 1861 to the Present (historic overview about the John Wanamaker Department Store).

Cahokia Courthouse, Illinois Historic Preservation Agency, March 1987 (brochure). September 1994 (brochure).

Cairo's Art Treasure, The Hewer (fact sheet). Includes exerpt from letter to Miss Adlaide Rendleman from George Grey Barnard on May 8, 1937.

Chicago House Wrecking Co. (Louisiana Purchase Exposition salvage catalogue).

Como Ordway Memorial Japanese Garden (St. Paul, MN) (brochure).

German Educational Exhibit, World's Fair, Saint Louis Missouri, 1904, Classical Sculpture exhibited by August Gerber, Cologne, Germany. Henry Rauth Printing Co. St. Louis, MO. (St. Louis Art Museum Library/Archives).

Germany, Lisa, *Historic Walking Tours, Texas State Cemetery.* Austin TX: Austin Convention and Visitors Bureau Historic Landmark Commission, 1995, pp. 22-23.

The Gorham Manufacturing Company, *Silversmiths and Goldsmiths.* Livermore & Knight Co., Providence, RI, 1904 (1904 Gorham LPE Exhibit Catalogue) St. Louis Public Library.

The Governor's Mansion, A Handclasp with History (brochure) (Jefferson City, Missouri).

Grant's Farm, Home of Mrs. August A. Busch, Sr. and Mr. and Mrs. August A. Busch, Jr. St. Louis County, Missouri. St. Louis, MO: Anheuser Busch, Inc, 1955.

The Great Organ, John Wanamaker Department Store, Philadelphia, PA (descriptive booklet).

The Haan House 1904-1994, St. Louis World's Fair 90th Anniversary Tour, October 15th-16th, 1994. Wabash Valley Trust for Historic Preservation, Lafayette, IN, 1994 (tour book).

Houck Collection Statuary Replicas . . . August Gerber, (UM-3-778 and UM-3 1283) (descriptive pamphlets), University Museum, Memorial Hall, Southeast Missouri State University.

An Invitation to Become a Friend of the Wanamaker Organ, John Wanamaker Department Store, Philadelphia, PA (descriptive brochure).

The Japanese Garden Seiwa-En (brochure) (Missouri Botanical Garden, St. Louis, Missouri).

Knutson, Jennifer. *Making History, Como Park Conservatory* (St. Paul, MN) (brochure – revised 8/1/96).

The 1990 Avery School Annual House Tour, Dec. 16th (descriptive tour pamphlet). Webster Groves, MO, 1990.

Phelps, Joe, ed. *Oklahoma Territory Building at the 1904 St. Louis Exposition* (historical pamphlet). El Reno Elks Lodge #743, El Reno, OK: 1989.

Regal Shoe Company Map.

St. Elizabeth of Hungary Catholic Church, Crestwood, MO (Self-guided tour brochure; letter dated February 2, 1986, from Rev. Ronald R. Tiefenbrunn, pastor, to parishioners; and narrative on life of St. Elizabeth of Hungary).

A Splendid Gift, Bulletin, State Normal School, December 1904, Cape Girardeau, Missouri (information paper on Gerber statuary collection including collection list).

The Swedish Homestead (commemorative postcard).

Tour of the Liberty Bell from St. Louis to Philadelphia, November 12 to 19, 1904. (INHP cat. No. 2369) (historical pamphlet from 1904 courtesy of the Independence National Historical Park, Philadelphia, PA).

Ulysses S. Grant (historic site brochure), Ulysses S. Grant National Historic Site, National Park Service, Department of the Interior (no date).

What to do at the Missouri Botanical Garden When It's Cold Outside (brochure) Missouri Botanical Garden (Fall/Winter 2000).

John L. Ziegenhein & Sons Funeral Homes (brochure).

ARCHIVES AND OTHER SOURCES

Affton (Missouri) Historical Society

Anheuser Busch Archives (correspondence)

Bradshaw, Betty Forney (interview on Moberly, MO gingko tree)

Brown, Kirby William (letter from Taxile Doat dated March 17, 1915 to William Victor Bragdon). Letter courtesy of Kirby William Brown, grandson of William Victor Bragdon

Browning, Gerald (correspondence on Moberly, MO gingko tree)

Buehler, Suzy, Oakland Historic Preservation Commission (West Virginia House)

Carnahan, Jean Senator (conversation 2000)

Cincinnati Art Museum

Clay County (Missouri) Historical Society (Historic Landmark plaque – Apollo House, Smithville, MO)

Cole County Historical Museum (Jefferson City, MO) (Francis desk)

The Corning Museum of Glass (Corning, NY)

Elisabet Ney Museum, Austin, TX

The Field Museum (Chicago, IL) (Collections records: Collections obtained by the Field Museum at the LPE (Louisiana Purchase Exposition)

Gaslight Square.org (Bruce Marren)

Glen Echo Country Club (Jim Healey, Golf Writer and Historian)

Hamilton, Esley, Preservation Historian, St. Louis County Parks

Illinois Historic Preservation Agency, Molly McKenzie, Site Manager, Cahokia Courthouse and Jarrot Mansion State Historic Sites

Madison County Historical Society (IL), Inc. (Ray Nicolaides Album, Gillham Family)

McPherson County Old Mill Museum and Park, Lindsborg, KS (Historical Evaluation from submission to Heritage Trust Fund Grant Program, Kansas Historical Society, 1997 and reference materials) (Lenora Lynam)

Mercantile Library, St. Louis

Milwaukee Public Museum

Minutes of the Board of Control of the Saint Louis School and Museum of Fine Arts, 1879-1908 (ref. pg. 202, letter dated December 13, 1905 to Wm. K. Bixby from Adolphus Busch re: St. Elizabeth Mosaics), The Washington University Archives

Missouri Botanical Garden (sculpture, signage and reference materials)

Missouri Historical Society Library and Archives
• Information Card File
• Letter dated March 13, 1905, to David R. Francis regarding restoration of Forest Park with item about the Minnesota granite shaft (Louisiana Purchase Exposition Company Collection, Box 24, Series XII, Subseries I, Folder 2)
• Awards – Department of Manufacturers (Louisiana Purchase Exposition Company Collection, Page

21, Box 7, Series III, Subseries IV, Folder 2)

Missouri Mansion Preservation, Inc. Jefferson City, MO (letter)

Mississippi River Museum, Dubuque, Iowa (snagboat exhibit information boards and letter)

New St. Marcus Cemetery, St. Louis, MO (Ziegenhein monument)

Parker, Jack (owner, OConnell's Restaurant)

Rhode Island School of Design (Providence)

Rock Island Arsenal (Rock Island, IL) (letter dated December 16, 1902, to The Chief of Ordnance, U.S. Army, Washington D.C. from the Major, Ord. Dept. at Rock Island Arsenal regarding items for display at the Louisiana Purchase Exposition and correspondence).

Rodin Musée, Paris, France

Sitka National Historic Park

Yale University Collection of Western Americana, Beinecke Rare Book and Manuscript Library. Letter dated September 3, 1903, from John Green Brady, Alaska Territorial Governor, to Thomas Ryan, Assistant Secretary of the Interior

Smithsonian Institution, Washington, D.C. Letters dated July 31, 1903 and August 10, 1903 from F.C.A. Richardson of the Milwaukee Papier Mache Works to F.A. Lucas, Smithsonian Institution – United States National Museum (Series 16, Louisiana Purchase Exposition, St. Louis, 1904, Correspondence 1901-1906)

Southeast Missouri State University Museum (staff tour)

St. Louis County Assessor's records

St. Louis Rowing Club Archives, Volume 1.

St. Louis Zoo (docent tour)

Texas State Cemetery Archives (Austin)

Thomas Jefferson, Epitaph, no date. Thomas Jefferson Papers. Library of Congress.

Toledo Museum of Art (Toledo, Ohio) (collections records)

Tower Grove Park (Friedrich Wilhelm von Steuben statue)

United States Department of the Interior, National Park Service, Independence National Historical Park, Philadelphia, PA (Liberty Bell)

University City Public Library and Archives (University City, Missouri) — Sue Rehkopf, Archivist, Historical Society of University City

University of Missouri – Columbia Archives

Washington University Ledger, Inventory of Property belonging to WU, (ref. pg. 60, St. Elizabeth Mosaics), The St. Louis Art Museum Archives

1904 World's Fair Society Archives

WEB SITES

The American Civil War, General Albert Sidney Johnston Tim Harrison & The Snuff Works website: http://www.swcivilwar.com/asjohnston.html

American National Biography On-line, "Heuduck, Paul Johannes, and Arno Paul Heuduck," by Robert Blaskiewicz: http://www.anb.org/articles/17/17-01676.html

Artnet Research Library: Dubois, Paul: http://www.artnet.com/library/02/0238/T023808.asp

Atascadero Education Foundation: http://www.aefkids.org/aefcityhistory.htm

Cincinnati Art Museum: http://www.cincinnatiartmuseum.org/greatart/tour_amerdecart.shtml

Georgia Magazine (The University of Georgia), "Remembering 'Charlie'" (An article about the late landscape architecture professor, Charlie Aguar, who co-authored *Wrightscapes, Frank Lloyd Wright's Landscape Designs*, with his wife, Berdeana) by Mary Jessica Hammes: http://www.uga.edu/gm/303/FeatCharlie.html

Grant's Farm Carriage Collection: http://www.grantsfarm.com/docs/car10.htm

Liberty Bell Museum, 1904 St. Louis World's Fair: http://www.libertybellmuseum.com/WorldsFair/1904.htm

Louisiana State Museum, The Cabildo, The Louisiana Purchase: http://lsm.crt.state.la.us/site/cabildo/cabildo.htm

Nebraska Department of Education John Gutzon Borglum (1871-1941): http://www.nde.state.ne.us/SS/notables/borglum.html

PBS On-line
American Experience, Mount Rushmore, Gallery, The Mares of Diomedes, 1904 http://www.pbs.org/wgbh/amex/rushmore/gallery/gal_rushmore_03.html
American Experience, Mount Rushmore, People & Events: Gutzon Borglum (1867-1941) http://www.pbs.org/wgbh/amex/rushmore/peopleevents/p_gborglum.html

Rock Island Arsenal Museum: http://riamwr.com/MuseumHist.htm

St. Louis Zoo, 1904 Flight Cage: http://www.stlzoo.org/

content.asp?page_name=FLTCAGE

Society of American Silversmiths – Other Silver Exhibitions & Events Magnificent, Marvelous Martelé, American Art Nouveau Silver, The Jolie and Robert Shelton Collection (November 10, 2001-January 13, 2002): http://www.silver smithing.com/1events.htm

Spencer Marks.com Fine Antiques, Silver & Books About Antiques http://www.spencermarks.com/ cgibin/webc.cgi/sz/ st_prod.html?p_prodid=1639

Springville Museum of Art John Gutzon Borglum: http:// www.shs.nebo.edu/Museum/ borglum.html

Smithsonian Institution, Washington, D.C. (Research Information System, Longview of American Painting and Sculpture, Inventories of American Painting and Sculpture): http://www.siris.si.edu

Ukiyo-e Gallery, "Frank Lloyd Wright, the Woodblock Print Collector," ©Thomas Crossland and Dr. Andreas Grund, March 2003: http://www.ukiyoe-gallery.com/flw.htm

US Army Corps of Engineers Brief History http:// www.hq.usace.army.mil/history/brief.htm

Virginia City, Nevada, History of Virginia City, Nevada and the Comstock Lode by Don Bush: http://www.vcnevada.com/history.htm

Yale-New Haven Teacher's Institute, Totem Poles of the North American Northwest Coast Indians by Maryanne Kathleen Basti: http://www.yale.edu/ynhti/curriculum/units/1985/6/85.06.01.x.html

Index

Symbols

1903 Osaka Exhibition 53
1904 Democratic Convention 64
1904 Olympic Games 27, 65, 125, 127
1904 World's Fair Society 107, 143

A

Adolphus Hotel 102
Affton, Missouri 46, 47
Alaska Territory Building 119
Albany Post Office 98
American Radiator Company 32
Anheuser-Busch 47, 101, 103
Apollo House 84
Apotheosis of St. Louis 35, 36
Archdiocese of St. Louis 110
Art Hill 13, 34, 35, 130, 131
Art nouveau 104
Atascadero, California 82, 83
Atlantic Pavilion 19

B

Barbe-Marbois, Francois Marquis De 68
Barnard, George Gray 85
Bauernhof Coach Room 101
Belgian Pavilion 102
Bethany College 56
Birmingham, Alabama 74, 75
Birmingham Steel and Iron Company 74
Bitter, Karl 68
Bixby Hall (Washington University) 95
Blanke, Cyrus 54
Boberg, Ferdinand 56
Borax Bill 37
Borglum, Gutzon 86
Brady, John Green 118, 138
British Pavilion 95
Brookings Hall 60, 95, 120
Brookings, Robert S. 60, 95, 120
Buffalo, New York 42
Busch, Adolphus 47, 62, 101

Busch, August A. Sr. 72, 78
Busch Hall 59, 62

C

C.F. Blanke Coffee Company 46
Cahokia Courthouse 38
Cahokia, Illinois 38
Cairo, Illinois 85
Cape Girardeau, Missouri 76
Carrington House 54
Catskill Mountains 52
Cella, Alexander 39
Centennial Exposition (1876) 16
Charleston, South Carolina 42
Chicago Centennial Commission 39
Chicago Historical Society 39
Chicago House Wrecking Company 11
China 12, 22, 24, 98, 101
Cincinnati Art Museum 104
Civilian Conservation Corps 119
Clayoquot tribesman 115
Cliff Road 31
Codman, William C. 104
Cole County Historical Museum 120
Columbian Exposition (1893) 16
Como Park 116, 117
Como-Ordway Japanese Memorial Garden 117
Conn, Luther 47
Connecticut State Pavilion 30
Corning Museum of Glass 114
Corps of Engineers 100
Creve Coeur Lake 126
Cupples Hall 59
Cupples, Samuel 62

D

David R. Francis Day 120
Davis, Henry G. 25
De Coubertin, Pierre 125
Department of Anthropology 25, 115
Department of Art 104
Department of Physical Culture 125

E

Eads Hall 61
Eads, James 61
Edison, Thomas 20
El Reno, Oklahoma 45
El Reno Oklahoma Elks Lodge #743 44

F

Festival Hall 11, 19, 22, 34, 67, 108, 130
Field Museum of Natural History 115
Flight Cage 48, 51, 130
Floral Clock 23, 106
Florentine Singer 87
Forest Devotion 78
Forest Park 11, 13, 16, 17, 50, 58, 69, 73, 111, 130
Forsyth, William 31
Fountain Angel 73
France 6, 16, 20, 24, 68
Francis, David R. 11, 12, 17, 18, 27, 34, 44, 65, 93, 111, 113, 120, 127
Francis Field 59, 65, 127
Francis Gymnasium 59, 65, 127
French, Daniel Chester 35
French Pavilion 102

G

Gaslight Square 95
Gates of Hell 70
Gaul, August 79
Gerber, August 76
Gerber-Houck Statuary 76, 77
German Country House 78
German Educational Exhibit 76
Germany 20, 24, 51, 72, 79, 81
Gilbert, Cass 34
Gingko Tree 105

gingko tree 72
Glen Echo Country Club 126
Gorham Manufacturing Company 104
Governor's Mansion (Missouri) 120
Grand Basin 13, 19, 68, 131
Grant, Fred D. 46
Grant, Julia Dent 46
Grant, Ulysses S. 46
Grant's Cabin 46
Grant's Farm 78, 101
Guilmant, Alexander 108
Gustaf, King Carl XVI 57

H

Haan-Potter Home 31
Halliday, Mary 85
Halliday, Captain William 85
Hardscrabble 46
Hearst, William Randolph 104
Hebrard, A. A. 70
Heuduck, Paul 110
Hinterseher, Josef 78
Hopkins, Arthur E. 71
Hot dog 27
Houck, Louis 76
How, Mrs. James Finney 61
Hymn of the West 19

I

Ice cream cone 6, 27, 75
Iced tea 27
Ikeda, Yoshitaka 53
Illinois Building 17
Independence Hall 112
Indiana Pavilion 31
Indianapolis, Indiana 119
Industrial Revolution 16
International Congresses 25, 58
International Golden Fossil Tree Society 105
International Olympic Committee 125

Still Shining

J

J.C. Nichols Company 88
Jackson Park, Chicago 39
Japan 20, 21, 52, 96, 98, 116
Japanese Eagle 88
Japanese Heritage Foundation 53
Japanese Imperial Garden 52, 96
Japanese lanterns 96
Japanese vase 89
Jefferson Guard 64
Jefferson Memorial 69, 130
Jefferson, Thomas 6, 25, 68, 92
Johnson Controls Company 106
Johnston, General Albert Sidney 80
Joy, Edward 47

K

Kansas City, Missouri 88, 108
Kessler, George 13
King Louis IX of France 35
Kirkwood, Missouri 51
Kwakiutl tribesmen 115

L

Lafayette, Indiana 30, 31
Lauchhammer, Germany 72
Lebosse, Henri 70
Lewis, Edward Garner 102
Lewis and Clark Exposition 119
Libbey Glass Company 114
Liberty Bell 112
Liggett Dormitory 59
Liggett, John E. and Elizabeth J. 63
Lindsborg, Kansas 57
Livingston, Robert 68
Lord & Taylor Department Store 109
Los Angeles Art Organ Company 108
Louisiana Purchase Exposition
    Company 58, 111, 114, 116
Lousiana Purchase 16, 60, 68
Lousiana Purchase Monument 68

M

Matthews, Leonard 96

McKinley, William 17
McWane, James R. 75
Metropolitan Museum of Art 71, 86
Milwaukee Papier Mache Works 124
Milwaukee Public Museum 119
Minnesota Shaft 111
Mississippi River 16, 100, 112
National Mississippi River Museum and
    Aquarium 100
Missouri Botanical Garden 73, 96
Missouri Building 121
Missouri History Museum 69, 107, 130
Missouri River 69
Moberly, Missouri 105
Monroe, James 68
Monticello, New York 52
Moretti, Giuseppe 74
Mormon Church 50
Museum of Science and Industry
    (Chicago, Illinois) 100

N

National Museum of Natural History
    124
National Postal Museum 99
National Register of Historic Places
    57, 103
New Orleans, Louisiana 68, 100
New St. Marcus Cemetery 122
Ney, Elisabet 80, 81
Niehaus, Charles H. 35

O

Oakland, Missouri 37, 41
Obelisk 21, 92, 94, 122
Observation Wheel 13, 26, 116
O'Connell's Pub 95
Ohio River 85
Oklahoma Day 44
Oklahoma Territory Pavilion 44
Olympic Games 27, 65, 125, 127
Olympic Regatta 126
O'Neil, Judge Joseph 73
Ortken, August 110
"Owney" 98

P

Pacific Pavilion 19
Painting 35, 130
Palace of Agriculture 23, 106
Palace of Art 34, 81, 86
Palace of Education and Social Economy
    20
Palace of Electricity 20
Palace of Forestry, Fish and Game 24
Palace of Horticulture 23
Palace of Liberal Arts 22, 76
Palace of Machinery 22
Palace of Manufactures 32
Palace of Mines and Metallurgy
    21, 37, 74
Palace of Pines and Maples 52
Palace of Transportation 21
Palace of Varied Industries
    21, 72, 78, 89, 110, 114
Pan-American Exposition 42
Paris Exposition Universelle 104
Park Lawn Cemetery 111
Parker, Alton B. 25
Pennsylvania Building 113
Pennsylvania Railroad Company 112
Peters, Charlotte 50
Petrilla 82
Philadelphia, Pennsylvania
    100, 108, 112
Philippine Insurrection weaponry 123
Philippine Village 24
Physical Culture Building 59, 65, 127
Pike 12, 19, 26
Pipe Organ 108
Plateau of States 39, 44, 121
Potter, William S. 30
Power Plant 22, 59
Press Building 42
Prince Hall 63
Prince Pu Lun 24, 101
Providence, Rhode Island 54, 104

R

Railway Mail Service 98
Ravenna Mosaic Company 110

Red Mountain 75
Rengen, John 54
Rhode Island Pavilion 54
Rhode Island School of Design 104
Ridgley Library 59, 64
River Des Peres 17
Rochester, New York 101
Rodin, Auguste 70, 86
Romanelli, Raffaello 73
Roosevelt, Theodore 18, 86, 129
Rubenstein, Helena 104
Ryan, Thomas 118

S

Saucier family 38
Schiffman, Rudolph 116
Schwanke-Kasten Jewelry Company
    107
Scientific American 114
Sculpture 35, 130
Sho-Fu-Den 53
Signing of the Treaty 68
Sigourney Mansion 30
Sitka National Historic Park 119
Smith, Stephen H. 54
Smithsonian Institution 24, 48, 124
Smithville, Missouri 84
Smoky Valley Historical Association 57
Snagboat Horatio G. Wright 100
Sousa, John Phillips 19
South Carolina Interstate and West
    Indian Exposition 42
Southeast Missouri State University 77
St. Clair County, Illinois 38
St. Elizabeth of Hungary Church 110
St. Louis Art Museum 35, 110, 130
St. Louis Municipal Opera 131
St. Louis Museum of Fine Arts 22
St. Louis Times Movie Review 111
St. Louis Typographical Union 8, 111
St. Louis Zoo 48, 130
St. Paul Foundry Company 48
St. Paul's Cemetery, St. Louis 47
St.-Gaudens, Louis 35
Staff 12, 18, 34, 35, 68, 130

Stegosaurus 24, 124
Sunset Memorial Park Cemetery 78

T

Takamine, Jokichi 52
Taylor, Isaac S. 121
Texas State Building 80
Texas State Cemetery 81
The Eagle 79
The Gulch 37
The Hewer 85
The Mares of Diomedes 86
The Muny 131
The Thinker 70
The World's Fair Bulletin 113
Thomas, W. W. Jr. 56
Three Fountains restaurant 95
Toledo Museum of Art 114
Totem Poles 115, 118
Tower Grove Park 72
Tower Hall 59, 63
Treasury Department 24
Tyrolean Alps 12

U

Umrath Hall 59, 63
United States Government Building 124
United States Mint 24
University City, Missouri 82, 127
University of Louisville 71
University of Missouri-Columbia 92
Utah State Pavilion 50

V

Valhalla Mausoleum 87
Vancouver Island, British Columbia 115
Vanderbilt, William 46
Virginia Day 92
Von Steuben, Baron Friedrich Wilhelm 72
Vulcan 74

W

Walters Art Gallery 71
Walters, Henry 71

Wanamaker, John 79, 108
War Department ordnance display 123
Washington State Pavilion 25
Washington University
        12, 17, 22, 25, 58, 60,
        95, 120, 127, 130
Water Nymphs 82
Webster Groves 33, 43, 47
Wells, Rolla 113
West Point Cadets 24
West Virginia State Pavilion 40
Western Iron Boat Building Company
        100
White Hall 30
William McKinley 17
Wisconsin State Pavilion 51
World's Fair Pavilion 121, 130
Wren, Christopher 95
Wrestling Bacchantes 82
Wright, Frank Lloyd 52

Z

Ziegenhein Funeral Home 89
Ziegenhein, Henry 122

Contacts

This book is just the "tip of the iceberg" of treasures remaining from the 1904 World's Fair. The author welcomes your comments and information on any splendid remnants from the fabulous fair.

Contact:
Diane Rademacher
c/o Virginia Publishing Co.
P.O. Box 4538
St. Louis, MO 63108

For information on other books by Virginia Publishing Company: www.stl-books.com

For information about the 1904 World's Fair Society in St. Louis:
1904 World's Fair Society
P.O. Box 440004
Brentwood, MO 63144
www.1904worldsfairsociety.org

(Stereoview: The Whiting View Comany #229) Author

Other titles from Virginia Publishing Company:

Made in USA: The Story of East St. Louis
Greg Freeman: A Gentleman, a Gentle Man
Spirits of St. Louis: A Ghostly Guide to the Mound City's Unearthly Activities
Wild Things: Untold Tales from the First Century of the Saint Louis Zoo
Beyond Gooey Butter Cake: Further Adventures in St. Louis Dining
Walking Historic Downtown St. Louis
Tales from the Coral Court
Legacies of the St. Louis World's Fair
Johnny Rabbit's 1001 St. Louis Trivia Questions
St. Louis Lost
The Streets of St. Louis: A History of St. Louis Street Names
Days and Nights of the Central West End

http://www.stl-books.com